MW00800478

THE COMPLETE GUIDE TO INSTALLING THE 44 SPLIT DEFENSE

Joe Roman

COACHES CHOICE™

ISBN: 1-57167-370-9
Library of Congress Catalog Card Number: 99-60472

Cover Design: Britt Johnson
Developmental Editor: David Hamburg
Production Manager: Michelle A. Summers

Coaches Choice Books is a division of: Sagamore Publishing, Inc.
P.O. Box 647
Champaign, IL 61824-0647
Web Site: http//www.sagamorepub.com

DEDICATION

To the memory of my brother, Robert Roman, sister Sharon Jacobson, and father, Joe Roman, Sr.; to my living sister Beverly Roman and mother, Peggy Roman. To all the young men who played football at the College of DuPage.

ACKNOWLEDGMENTS

I am grateful to the many coaches I have worked with and thank them for their friendship. Particularly, I would like to thank our head coach, Bob MacDougall, for both giving me the opportunity to coach and teaching me how to coach.

CONTENTS

I arrived at the College of DuPage in 1975 as the defensive coordinator and held this position for 23 years. From the beginning, our base defense was the "44 Split." During those 23 years, our teams won 75 percent of their games (182-61). During that time, we suffered only one losing season. We also played in 14 bowl games and won 10 of them. In addition, we won 12 state junior college championships and set the National Junior College Athletic Association record for consecutive victories with 36.

From 1986 to 1996, the College of DuPage was 107-22. We won eight consecutive state championships and were ranked in the top 10 in the nation seven times, finishing second twice and fourth three times. During the same time period, our team defense was rated among the top 10 in the country eight times. In 1995, our best year for team defense, we were ranked No. 1 in the nation in team defense. That season, we gave up a total of 51 points in 12 games, for an average of 4.25 points per game. Our opponents averaged 132 yards in total offense per game—35 yards rushing and 97 yards passing. For three seasons, in the midst of our 36-game winning streak, our opponents averaged 5.9 points per game and 179 yards in total offense per game.

Great football programs are measured by more than their won-lost record. On average, 92 percent of our sophomores received scholarships to universities and colleges. Some of those athletes went on to play in the NFL, while others finished school and entered the professional workforce in a wide spectrum of professions. We also enjoyed a number of intangible "wins," as many a young man learned something about the value of hard work and discipline through our program. Championship-caliber statistics, memorable achievements, and the personal "wins" of our players all indicate our overall success as a winning football program.

This book describes our particular formula for success, with an emphasis on the defensive side of the football. Any good coach will tell you that the success of a football program is based on several factors, beginning with a group of committed, talented professionals. Undoubtedly, the College of DuPage had a great football program, thanks to the dedicated work of our head coach, Bob MacDougall. The College of DuPage employed a group of talented and committed coaches who put their own unique stamp of technique and leadership on both the offense and the defense. I learned a great deal from them. I am a better coach and person because of people like Bob MacDougall, Bill Duchon, John Persons, Ken Mills, Tim Heinrich, Randy McCue, Ed Miller, Darryl Richardson, John Urban, Tom Minnick, Gene Benhart, Scott Kellar, and Matt Foster, just to name a few.

We also had some outstanding athletes play for us. Having great athletes on your team doesn't always make for a great team. You must have the ability to put the athlete in the best position to make the play. If we were successful as a defensive team, it was primarily because of our players and the defense we used, the "44 Split." We faced every type of offense from the wishbone to the run-and-shoot, and we were able to stop those offenses by playing our base defense.

Making the Choice

The most important thing you can do when selecting a defense is to make a commitment to one defensive alignment. As the coach, you must make it clear to your players and your fellow coaches that the defense you have chosen is the defense you are going to hang your hat on. You and your players must be confident that no matter what type of offense you face, your base defense will be able to stop it.

In order to properly install your base defense, you must teach it to your athletes on each of three different levels: individual, unit, and team. However, before moving on to other alignments, stunts, and coverages of the base defense, you must make sure your players understand their individual responsibilities, including their alignments, their keys, and their assignments. On any football team, every defensive player must know the responsibilities of each defensive unit (the front, the linebackers, and the secondary) and how those units come together as a whole defensive team. With this approach to defense, you can overcome any shortcomings your players may have.

During my 23 years at the College of DuPage, I regularly explained my defensive philosophy to my players by using the following military analogy: Near the end of World War II, the U.S. Army Air Force was responsible for making bombing runs over Germany. These raids occurred during the daylight hours, which made the bombers easy targets for German fighter planes. For a while, the U.S. bombers suffered heavy losses to German fighter planes until the U.S. started using a new airplane, the B-29 "Flying Fortress." This plane had three times the number of machine guns as the old planes, and it also had gun mounts in its undercarriage. When the B-29s flew in a formation, the fire from all their machine guns made it impossible for the German fighters to get to the B-29s without themselves getting shot down. However, whenever one of those U.S. bombers broke from the formation, it was left vulnerable to attack by the German fighters and also weakened the B-29 formation. What kept the U.S. bombers effective was that everybody in the bomber had a job and every bomber had a place in the formation. It was a life-or-death proposition. Like the crew member of a B-29, each defensive player has a job to do. The defensive units—the front, the linebackers, and the secondary—must control their positions in the overall defensive formation. The success of the overall defense depends on the ability of eleven players to act as one.

When you prepare your team for an opponent, your base defense is the defense you prep. I cannot recall, for instance, a single game when we did not prep our players to beat a team by using our base defense. We always presented adjustments, stunts, coverages, and fronts as a means of taking advantage of an opponent's weakness. Your base defense should be the foundation on which all of your stunts, coverages, fronts, and adjustments, as well as your game plan, are built. This base defense is your "island in a storm" when things are going badly for you. If for some reason your opponent is on a roll and your game plan is a bust and you need to restart your attack, you must go back to the starting point, which is the defense your players know best—your base defense.

As a coach who is committed to his defensive system, it is important that you instill that system in your players' minds before you begin to expand your defensive package. Your defense should never become a smoke-and-mirrors defense. Too often, I have observed coaches who either change their defense every week or abandon their base defense so they can make an adjustment that they think will stop an opponent in a particular situation—without even giving their base defense a chance to show what it can do. What kind of message are you sending to your players when you desert the defense you've been teaching them since the beginning of the season, and where do you turn when your alternative plan fails?

What you as a coach should understand is that when your players know their roles within your base defensive scheme, any adjustments you may have to make during the course of a game involve simple transition. You must be ready and able to adjust your defense during a game in order to meet and change the momentum of your opponent's attack. At the College of DuPage, we often had to make adjustments in certain situations that were not in our game plan or our playbook. The ability of your players to adapt to special circumstances is possible only if they have a total understanding of the defense. That flexibility is the mark of a great defensive package.

CHAPTER 2

The 44 Split Defense

When building a championship football program, you should start with your defense. Offense wins games; defense wins championships. Clearly, it is your defense that must rise to the occasion every week to stop the opposing offense; if it fails to get the job done, then your team will not be able to beat the opposition. In order to work properly, your defensive scheme must be effective, versatile, and easy to teach. As a coach, you must keep in mind that it is your athletes who are the ones who actually play the game; consequently, it makes absolutely no difference what you know about your defense if your players don't understand it.

The subject of this book, the 44 Split defense, meets all the criteria of a defense that will make your team a champion. At the College of DuPage, we found the 44 Split to be a balanced defense that lends itself to easy alignments and adjustments. Most important, it is a defense that is effective against all offensive schemes.

The question most often asked by coaches who were curious about our defense was "What are your reasons for using this defense?" My answer was always the same: The alignment is simple, the defensive personnel are readily available on any football team, and it is easy to teach. I cautioned, however, that defensive players need to know three components of defensive football before they can be accomplished at playing the 44 Split: alignments, assignments, and keys. If players can't get the alignment right, then they may as well forget about the other two. At all levels of football, from high school to professional, defensive mistakes in alignment are turned into offensive touchdowns. If you don't believe me, get out your game film and have a look. A good deal of your opponent's offensive scheme and game plan are devoted to getting your defense to misalign by keeping it off guard with an assortment of formations, motion ploys, and the shift of formations.

Once you choose the 44 Split as your defensive alignment, your problems will be cut in half. The 44 Split is a balanced defense that uses five defenders on one side of the ball and five on the other side, with the safety in the middle of the formation. A good safety with range, who can bring it to either side, gives your defense the flavor of Canadian football, where you have twelve players on a side. The 44 Split defense is strong against the run, both in the middle and to the outside. It covers the passing zones with four linebackers under and a three-deep secondary. Neither the run nor the pass strength of this defense is compromised by how the offense uses the field. It does not matter whether the offense deploys formations that stretch the defense or uses motion to change the offensive alignment. Our adjustment to offensive formations, including the movement of receivers and backs, involves a simple widening or shortening in the alignment of one or two players.

The kind of personnel you need in order to run a 44 Split defense are usually on hand on almost all football teams. The undersized overachiever always seem to find a spot on this defense, and as it turns out, every team seems to have an abundance of those undersized linebackers; bigger, slower defensive backs; or fullback and tailback rejects. In fact, six of the eleven positions in the 44 Split are best filled by linebacker types of players.

The most important quality we looked for, of course, was speed. Since speed can destroy the opposition, coaches must first look for athletes who can run. If they can't run, whatever size advantage they have is useless. In the 44 Split, the two tackles are the only players who line up in a four-point stance and therefore are usually the only defensive players in this system who have considerable size.

The 44 Split defense does not require players to fill what are known as "tweener" positions, such as the drop end, whose responsibilities may include rushing the passer or dropping into coverage. Another example of a "tweener" position is the strong safety, who is called upon to provide primary run support or deep pass coverage in other situations. These types of positions are difficult to coach and to play. They cause problems in practice scheduling during run and pass breakdown time. For example, if the defensive front is working on pass rush and linebackers, while the linebackers and the secondary are working on pass drops, to which group do you send the drop end? If the secondary is working on pass-coverage alignment, and the run-support players are working on option coverage, where do you send the strong safety? These "tweener" players end up getting only half the coaching that the other players get.

With the 44 Split, teaching the defense is simplified by the breakdown of units and the similarities between the weakside and strongside positions. If you have three coaches on your defensive staff, the ideal unit breakdown is as follows: defensive front (ends and tackles), linebackers (outside and inside), and secondary (halfbacks and safety). Also, in a three-coach scenario, the defensive coordinator should be the one who coaches the linebackers. At times, I have successfully coached the defense with two defensive coaches. If you have only two defensive coaches, the coordinator should coach the linebackers and front, and the other coach should oversee the secondary.

The similarities in alignments, assignments, and keys between the weakside and strongside positions make them interchangeable. A weakside end, for example, would have no problem playing the strongside end. The similarities also make the units flexible, which increases the opportunities for teaching. When breaking the defense down for group work, for instance, you are not confined to the standard breakdown of defensive line, linebacker, and secondary. During unit work, the balance of the defense makes it possible to mix positions in a variety of ways, such as the inside linebackers and the tackles working on trap plays; the outside linebackers and the ends working on option plays; the secondary working on three-deep coverage; the ends, the tackles, and the inside linebackers working on run and stunts; and the outside linebackers and secondary working on two-deep coverage and alignment. In addition to a better teaching environment, the unit work provides an opportunity for the players to work in small groups consisting of a wider range of defensive positions than their own. This opportunity makes for a better understanding and knowledge of the total defense. It supports the transitions of players from one position to another (outside linebacker to end, or halfback to outside linebacker).

The manner in which the players in the 44 Split are instructed to home in on either the run or the pass provides them with a clear progression to follow: The defensive front plays run first, then looks to rush and contain the passer. The linebackers also play run first and then react to pass. The under coverage is a pattern read that is simple and also makes it easy to find receivers in the under-coverage zones. The secondary plays pass first. It has no primary support on either the option or the run.

Other advantages of the 44 Split defense include the following:

- It gives your defense the ability to run a variety of stunts, defensive fronts, and coverages without changing personnel.

- It confuses the opponent and disrupts its offensive blocking schemes.

- Its strength is stopping the run and containing the pass.

- It requires a balanced alignment, which in turn gives every player a great angle to the ball.

Thanks to the 44 Split defense, during our 36-game winning streak at the College of DuPage, it was a rarity for our opponents to break a play for more than a 20-yard gain.

CHAPTER 3

Personnel

Football players come in all shapes and sizes, so it would be foolish to suggest that a player's height, weight, or speed might prohibit him from playing a particular position. Granted, a lack of physical attributes would make it difficult for some players to fill certain defensive positions, but it would be a mistake to sell a kid short before you can see what he can do under fire. One of our best-ever defensive tackles at DuPage was 6'1", 215 pounds, but he was special. We also had an inside linebacker who was so slow, I wouldn't let him run a 40-yard dash on test day because I didn't want to know just how slow he was. Nevertheless, he had great anticipation, as well as the ability to knock ball carriers on their backs. He was 4.7 on game day.

STRONG AND WEAK ENDS

When looking for athletes to fill the defensive end position, the physical attributes to look for are speed and height. Our defensive ends, on average, weighed between 210 and 230 pounds and stood from 6' to 6'4" tall. Most often, former high school inside or outside linebackers are the best fit at the defensive end position. Speed and size will determine who will play either the strongside or the weakside defensive end. The strongside end aligns on the tight end side of the offensive formation. This alignment will make the strong end the widest defender on the strong side. When it comes to choosing a strong end, you should place more importance on speed than on size. The reason is that the strong end's alignment puts him at a greater distance from the quarterback's pass-drop point, making speed more important than size at that position. Because of the strong end's wide alignment, he is rarely subjected to trap blocks and, consequently, does not need the size that is necessary when taking on trap blocks. The weak end will be blocked by offensive guards and tackles, which makes size more important for a player at that position. The slower of the two ends should play the weak side, because his alignment is nearer to the ball, which means that the distance he will have to travel in order to reach the quarterback's pass-drop point will be shorter than that of the strongside end. Although these end positions are taught as strongside end and weakside end, you can teach them as left end and right end, as long as both players are equally fast.

RIGHT AND LEFT TACKLE

In the 44 Split, your defensive tackles are the cornerstone of your defense. The defensive tackles must have quickness and size (not to be confused with speed and height). When assessing quickness, a 40 time can be misleading. Forty yards is a long haul for a big kid. At DuPage, we incorporated an agility drill we called the "Pro Agility" and vertical jump to evaluate quickness. The Pro Agility is a 20-yard agility run completed over a 10-yard course. Three cones are placed on a line that's 10 yards long, one on each end and one in the middle. The athlete starts at the middle cone and, on command, sprints to the cone on the right, then sprints to the cone on the left, and then sprints back to the middle. If his time for the "Pro Agility" is more than five-tenths of a second faster than his time in the 40, it is an indication that the athlete possesses quickness.

On the basis of years of experience, we determined that tall athletes have a hard time playing defensive tackle. Height can be a hindrance to a defensive tackle, particularly if his height keeps him from playing low. We found that the ideal height for a defensive tackle is in the range of 6' to 6'4"; any taller, and the player tends to lose leverage. The preferred weight for the tackle will depend on his ability to move, yet still have enough body weight to prevent him from getting knocked off the ball. The tackle must be able to control the offensive guard and the line of scrimmage. Your best tackle should play at left defensive tackle. When your defensive tackles are good, they improve the play at the other positions.

SAM LINEBACKER

The Sam linebacker is to the 44 Split defense what a power forward is to a basketball team. Sam must be one of your best athletes. He must have the athletic ability to play the pass, plus the physical size and quickness to take on the blocks of offensive linemen. He ought to be able to strike a blow from an upright position and read multiple keys. It takes more time to develop a Sam linebacker than it does to develop a player at any other linebacker position. We played an athlete who was undersized at this position, but he had the combination of great quickness and a good football mind. A good Sam linebacker will cause offenses a lot of problems.

MIKE AND MEG LINEBACKERS

Our linebackers pilot our overall defense, and our inside linebackers lead our linebacker corps. The Mike linebacker plays on the strong side of the defense. Mike, as a rule, is the bigger and slower of the two inside linebackers; he can get away with a lack of speed because, with the strong end and the Sam linebacker playing on the line of scrimmage, the Mike linebacker will have more help to the outside. He is more of a plug linebacker than Meg is. The Meg linebacker should be faster than the Mike linebacker and also better at playing the pass. He will have more open ground to cover than Mike will.

For you, the coach, the first consideration when selecting a linebacker is his ability to get off of blocks and make the tackle. As far as on-field leadership is concerned, you should leave the decision making to the inside linebackers. On game day, they are your voice on the field. Size and speed are a bonus, but these attributes should not take preference over the ability of the linebacker to get to the ball.

SARA LINEBACKER

The Sara linebacker is the weakside outside linebacker. When looking to fill this position, the first attribute you should look for is a linebacker who is comfortable playing in space. The Sara linebacker position is very similar to a strong safety position, except that the player who assumes this role will not have to go into any kind of deep pass coverage. The Sara linebacker should be your most athletic linebacker. He must be adept at playing the pass, and he must also be a good open-field tackler.

SECONDARY

The defensive halfbacks and the safety need to be specialists at playing the pass. Although speed and height are qualities that everyone looks for in defensive backs, above all, they must be good athletes. The athlete you should be looking for in the secondary must have the capacity to backpedal, flip turn, break on the ball, and tackle in the open field. The safety is usually a team's best athlete. He does not need to be as fast as the halfbacks, but he does need to have enough range so he can move and break on the ball. The safety is to football what the center fielder is to baseball. If you can find a defensive back who hits like a linebacker and gets a great break on the ball, you should make him your safety.

CHAPTER 4

What We Do Differently

We at the College of DuPage did not invent the 44 Split defense. As a young coach, my knowledge of football at the college level was limited, but I did understand that there was more to defensive football than a good pregame speech. When Bob MacDougall came to DuPage as the head football coach, he inherited me as a defensive coordinator, and we have been together for 22 years. Bob has been a great friend, a wonderful teacher, and an understanding head coach to work for. Bob brought the Notre Dame 44 Split defense with him from Michigan Tech University, where he was the defensive coordinator. I tried to learn everything I could about the 44 Split defense from Bob and anyone else who would talk to me about it. The defense was popular during the 1950s; it was an effective response to option-type offenses. Variations of the 44 Split were the Wide Tackle 6 and the 46 defense, both of which have also made a comeback. In the 44 Split, teams played a lot of man coverage, which caused them problems. It was hard to find athletes who could play man coverage, and when the offense broke a play, it usually went all the way for a touchdown.

At the College of DuPage, if we had a unique scheme or approach to teaching this defense, it would have to be in the way we presented it to our athletes. For 23 years, the first and last thing a College of DuPage football player heard from the coaches was "Do the little things right and the big things will be taken care of." The point we wanted to drive home was that the players must understand the first step—and get it right—before they even think about what comes next. We found that when we were demanding with the details, our players became disciplined in their approach to learning and playing the 44 Split defense. As teachers, we coaches did not progress from one defensive skill to another until the players mastered the skill we were working on. We have gone into games with only our base defense, one coverage, and two stunts as a defensive package, because that was all we could do at that particular point in the season.

TEACHING THE DEFENSE

The key to teaching any defense is making the defense simple enough for the players to grasp it, while allowing the coaches the opportunity to mix complex alignments, stunts, and coverages. Once your players have an understanding of their individual techniques, alignments, assignments, and keys, you should then move to the next step. As they become familiar and comfortable with the 44 Split, your players must understand how their position is related to and interacts with all the other positions around them. In other words, they should first see the "small world" and then see the "big world." Your players should start to continuously communicate with one another, relaying option, run, and pass responsibilities, as well as strength, receiver sets, and backfield sets. The 44 Split is a gap-control defense in which each player has a gap that is his primary run responsibility. The defense against the option play is broken down into three parts: #1 dive, #2 quarterback, and #3 pitch. The defense against the pass is also broken down into three different areas of responsibility: rush, contain, and a pass coverage zone.

Before each play, it is the responsibility of every player to tell his teammates on either side of him and behind him what their run, option, and pass responsibilities are. (This double-checking for knowledge and understanding is a basic skill in teaching and learning.) By repeating the various run, option, and pass assignments to one another, the players have a means of checking each other, thereby increasing the possibility of eliminating mistakes in alignment and assignment (e.g., "I've got #2, C, and contain," "I've got #1, A, and hook to curl"). When the players become comfortable with both the base defense and their position, the different defensive fronts, stunts, and coverages can be taught as an adjustment to the base defense. Thus the defense becomes a well-oiled machine with interchangeable parts. As a coach, you can therefore strive for unlimited possibilities. Since you can make these adjustments and game plans simple for your players—and as long as the players understand their responsibilities—you and your staff can orchestrate the defense of your choosing. At the College of DuPage, we called two different fronts; we ran one on the weak side and the other on the strong side. You, too, can call two different stunts, coverages, or fronts and also have the option to run the one of your choice, depending on what type of formation the offense uses. You can also do what we did at DuPage, that is, make up a new defensive front during a game in order to stop an offensive charge. We could do it rather easily, because we started from a simple base in which each player knew his position, as well as the positions of the other players, and was adept at communicating with his teammates.

STRENGTH CALLS

When putting together a defensive package, you must determine how you will deploy your defense against the offensive formation you are facing. We will identify the run and pass strength of an offensive formation by making two strength calls— one to the run and the other to the pass. Specifically, we will employ two types of strength calls: (1) Make a strength call to the tight end side of the offensive formation, where the tight end can serve as an extra blocker on a running play. (2) Make a strength call to the two-receiver side of the offensive formation, which would align the defense to the passing strength of the offensive formation. The idea is to match strength against strength. The purpose of the strength call is to keep the defense balanced by deploying the eleventh defender to the run or pass strength of the offensive formation. The strength call is also used to direct the movement of the defense just prior to or after the snap of the ball. The strength call gives direction to your fronts, stunts, and coverages.

At DuPage, after analyzing the two most common types of strength calls, we saw an opportunity to double our options in the movement of the defense and a means of preventing offenses from restricting our defensive package through the use of different formations. Our defense had six positions that could align toward or away from the strength call, while the other five positions remained relatively unaffected. We make the "strength call" to the tight end side of the offensive formation. Keep in mind that the eleventh man is the safety who aligns in the middle of the offensive formation (which is usually a few yards to one or the other side of the ball).

The 44 Split alignment is balanced to begin with; thus the strength call will put your strongside players, who are better suited to play the run, to the tight end side of the offensive formation. Your weakside players, who are better at playing the pass, will go to the split end side of the offensive formation. You then make a second strength call, which will be to the two-receiver side, alerting the defense to the passing strength of the offensive formation. It is recommended that you use a color to identify the second strength call. At DuPage, we had the strongside inside linebacker make the strength call: "Strong right! Strong right!" After the strength call, the safety and the halfbacks made the color call: "Brown left! Brown left!" The benefit of making the two strength calls is well worth the time it takes to put them in. The concept is quickly picked up by the players, which increases their awareness of both the run and the pass strengths of the offensive formation.

As a rule, your defensive front has no problem seeing the "small world," but sometimes it has trouble bringing the "big world" into focus. By making two strength calls, the players on the defensive front become more aware of total offensive deployment and how it affects them. In addition, your game plans and adjustments become enhanced by the opening up of more opportunities to take advantage of offensive tendencies. At DuPage, we were able to employ different combinations of defensive fronts, stunts, and coverages. Any number of defensive fronts, stunts, or coverages can be called to attack either the run or the pass strength of an offensive formation. If you wanted to put pressure on the passer by stunting, for example, you could call two stunts and then run just one of those stunts to one receiver side. You could also call two different fronts and then align in the defensive front that best matches the run strength of the offensive formation. The upshot is that by identifying run and pass strengths, you are able to be more complex with your defense, while keeping it simple for your athletes.

COMMUNICATION

Physical errors will never beat you if your team is playing good team defense, but mental errors will kill you. Rarely will you see a football game lost because of a physical mismatch; most often, the winner is the team that makes the fewest mistakes. Offensive errors may stop a drive or a score, but seldom do they result in a score for the opponent. The defense does not have the luxury of making a mistake. A defensive mistake shows up when you least expect it. These errors made by coaches and players are most often turned into touchdowns by the offense. It is the defense's job to keep the opponent out of the end zone. Mental mistakes are made because of a lack of focus and communication. In order to prevent mental errors, you must develop and practice the skill of game communication. This skill must be mastered and worked on every day. During the course of a game, you must be able to make adjustments to your defense, evaluate the play of your players, and analyze the attack of the offense. Defensive football is a game of reaction. The conscious thought occurs only before the snap and after the whistle—everything in between is reaction.

A football game is played in what seems like seconds. During a game, when you are trying to make an adjustment, time and words are in short supply. The communicating must occur quickly and on three levels: (1) from player to player, (2) from player to coach, and (3) from coach to coach. These lines of communication must be two-way, and there cannot be a breakdown at any level.

As a defensive coordinator, you should be a collector of information and not a dictator. You would be foolhardy to cut off any source of information. You need listen to, evaluate, and coordinate all information from players and coaches. When you meet with your coaches, you should expect input and listen to what they have to say about the defense. For his part, each player must have a feeling of ownership in the defense and know that his opinions are worthwhile. I have had some great game adjustments come from the input of a player.

I would tell my players that they must learn a new language, that they will be speaking in "football shorthand." A word, a number, or a phrase must be able to trigger what would take sentences and paragraphs to say. We liked to use catchwords that key a response to either alignment, technique, or a blocking scheme. When possible, we preferred to keep the explanation of an offensive play, an area of responsibility, or a technique to one word or number labels. When we wanted to refer to an offensive blocking scheme, we would give it a name that told the player what gap the play was going to, who was going to carry the ball, and what the blocking scheme (ice, power, tear) was to be.

Every defensive player should have an offensive position he will play on the "prep team." (At DuPage, we did not rely on the offense to be our "scout team.") The

defensive player should be responsible for the offensive position that will most often be blocking him: The inside linebackers must know the center and the fullback positions (the strongside inside linebacker becomes the center, and the weakside inside linebacker becomes the fullback). The defensive tackles are the offensive guards, and the defensive ends are the offensive tackles. The outside linebackers are the tight end and the tailback (specifically, the strongside outside linebacker is the tight end, and the weakside outside linebacker is the tailback). The two halfbacks are the wide receivers, and the safety is the quarterback. Each player must know the blocking schemes and assignment for the different offensive plays.

When we were working on team time, our second defense was our offensive scout team, but everyone took his turn on the scout squad. We had the scout team wear a jersey with the same number as the player who was to play the position for our opponent. We had a complete set of numbered jerseys that could be put on and taken off quickly. This system allowed us to pick up tendencies in substitutions, special plays, blocking schemes, and the roles of key players. In order to run the opponent's offensive play, all the coach needed to say was "Blue right, split backs, tear weak," and the scout team would know how to run this play. We found this method of running team time to be very useful in many ways.

Once you subscribe to this same system, your players will learn offensive plays, blocking schemes, and formations much more quickly. The players see the offensive plays from both sides of the line of scrimmage and have a good understanding of the opponent's offense. When discussing the offensive attack on game day, it reduces the need for verbal communication. Time is very important, and the last thing you need is a long explanation of an offensive play. When you say, "Ice," "Tear," "Power," or "Base," the players will have an image of an entire offensive play. Likewise, if you say, "Brown left," the players will have a mental picture of an offensive formation with a tight end on the right side, two split wide receivers to the left side, and the "strength" to the right.

Whenever you change the defensive formation or run a stunt, you will force a change in some of the players' option, gap, and pass responsibilities. As previously mentioned, the players must relay to one another their option, gap, and pass responsibilities. If two players come up with the same number for their option responsibility, they will automatically know something is wrong and be able to correct their respective responsibilities.

We made it a point to work on communication when body fatigue began to set in. You probably have heard the saying, "Fatigue makes cowards of us all." Actually, fatigue makes us stupid. If you think back, you surely can recall a time when one of your best and most dependable players made a mental error toward the end of a hard-fought game. The mental error was made because the athlete's body reached a fatigue level where he was unable to concentrate on his assignment. At the end of practice, when we ran sprints, we would break down into our individual units. The players would align in their defensive stance, and the coach would check those stances. One of five commands—pass, ball, screen, draw, trap—was given to the players. On that command, they would react to ball movement and yell out the command as they left the starting line. The end of practice is when players start to lose their concentration. We found that that was the best time to practice on their focus by installing a discipline that they would be able to call upon during a game.

TRAPPING THE BALL

When coaches tell their players that they need great pursuit to the football, they are not actually relaying the correct meaning of "pursuit." The word *pursuit* is defined in the dictionary as an attempt to "follow in an effort to overtake or chase." What you actually want your players to do when they pursue is to trap and contain the ball carrier. True pursuit is a skill that your players need to be taught. You can best teach your defense how to learn pursuit by using a progression of tackling drills, starting with individual tackling techniques and ending with team tackling. The purpose of these drills is to teach the players how to tackle, how to close quickly on an angle that forces the ball carrier to redirect, and how to work together to trap the ball carrier. As a player, I can remember hearing our coach say, when he was teaching pursuit, "Never follow the same color jersey." Think about it, though. How does that instruction help a player take a proper angle to the ball carrier? You must face the fact that there will be times when an athlete of lesser ability is going to be asked to tackle an athlete of superior ability. That lesser athlete needs a more concrete plan than a reminder never to follow the same jersey.

The first step is to teach your players to take a direct angle to the ball carrier and to then close on that angle at full speed. The angle should be aimed at one of three points, which will depend on the tackler's approach angle to the ball: outside shoulder, head-up, and back hip. The tackler should close quickly on the ball carrier, forcing him to either run into the tackler or redirect. When you think about it, a ball carrier has only three options: straight, right, or left. Therefore, it is not a good idea to give the ball carrier either the time or the opportunity to work on the tackler. The ideal approach is for the tackler to take an angle that will take away two of the ball carrier's options. When closing from the outside, the tackler should run at the outside shoulder of the runner, forcing the runner to choose the inside. If the tackler's teammate is at his proper angle of attack, the ball carrier will be trapped and contained. The progression of teaching is on four levels: individual, unit, group, and team. When you teach the importance of tackling within the context of a team plan and work together to take away all of the ball carrier's options by the angles of approach, it's eleven against one, and everyone is trapping the guy with the ball.

PASS COVERAGE AND PATTERN READ

Your philosophy on pass defense in the 44 Split is simple: Never get beat deep. At the College of DuPage, we played a three-deep zone defense. As a change-up or adjustment, we ran some two- and four-deep zone. Our under coverage consisted of six zones, and we would "pattern read" in these underneath zones. We ran some five under zones and "man" coverages. Our deep coverage was never less than two deep. We never ran any "man free" or total "man" coverage, because those types of coverages can produce one-play touchdown drives. We tried to keep it simple. Our defensive backs stayed on top of all deep routes and would break on and contain all other routes. Our under coverage, the linebackers, played under the deepest receiver in their zone and broke up on short routes. When talking to our players about pass coverage, we stressed three important points:

- **Panic is your biggest enemy.** Have confidence in yourself, the defense, and your teammates. A completed pass does not spell the end. The odds are on your side. Even if the opponent has a great passer, he will only complete a little more than half his passes.

- **Break on the ball and contain it**. Trap the ball. Make the receiver pay the price and do it at full speed. When you're going full speed on a good angle to the ball, you make things happen. In most pass plays broken up by a defender, the ball was in the receiver's hands. A good break on the ball will get you there in time to make the receiver cough up the ball.

- **Keep in mind the concept of "small world, big world."** Focus on your key, get a run or pass read quickly, and then open your vision and see the full picture.

We always numbered the receivers from the inside out. The No. 1 receiver was the first receiver on or off the line of scrimmage who was nearest the ball. (Since we did not number across the formation, there were No. 1 receivers on both sides of the offensive formation.) The No. 2 receiver was the next receiver to the outside. If there was only one receiver to a side, No. 2 would be a back in the backfield or a player running a pass route, who was coming from the opposite side of the offensive formation. The No. 3 receiver on either side would be one of two possibilities—the third receiver to the outside on or off the line of scrimmage, or the back coming out of the backfield on a pass route (or on a pass route from the opposite side of the formation).

Our under coverage was a pattern read system—a matchup zone defense. We played man coverage on the deepest route in the zone and would break up on the short routes in the zone. When pass showed, the linebacker found the deepest receiver in the zone who was his responsibility and locked on him until the receiver cleared the zone. When the linebacker located the receiver, he kept his eyes on the receiver and didn't look back at the quarterback until the receiver made his cut or ran out of the zone. The order in which the linebacker would look for receivers was (1) the receivers to his side, (2) those running routes from his opposite side, and (3) backs running routes out of the backfield.

Catchwords and analogies are useful tools in helping players learn. The mention of a word or a phrase can key a response that an entire paragraph couldn't succeed in evoking. I found, for example, that if I took time out of practice to tell a joke or a story, the players would hang on every word. Keep in mind that no matter how stupid the joke or story may be, your players will remember it—more important, they will remember the message.

When teaching our pattern read under coverage, I used the following analogy: For some reason, you and a friend are approached by five individuals who want to fight you and your friend. There is a lot of talking, but you see that not all of them will come right at you. You figure it would be to your advantage to divide them into two groups: those who will attack first and those who will sneak around and jump you while you're not looking (bullies and rats). The bullies are the guys doing all the talking and are the most conspicuous (receivers). The rats are the guys you must look out for; they will be the guys who will come at you while you're not looking (receivers from the opposite side and backs running routes). When pass shows, find the bullies and look for the first one to your outside while you move toward him. If No. 1 runs out of your zone, look for the second bully (if there are two receivers to your side). If the bullies do not run a route in your zone, then pull up, look for the rats at your back (first, those on crossing routes from the opposite side and, second, backs running routes out of the backfield). The linebacker's eyes should not be locked on the receiver throughout the entire play. When the receiver makes his cut, the linebacker should look back for the ball and the quarterback. If the receiver runs out of the zone, the linebacker should pull up, and look for rats, then the ball, and, finally, to the quarterback. In actuality, pass coverage is not this simple, but if you can make a part of it simple by using a corny analogy, players will respond.

We used pattern read as our under coverage for 15 years and would never have gone back to a straight drop coverage. Straight drop coverage is the conventional linebacker means of dropping to an area and keying the front shoulder of the quarterback, along with his release, while getting a good break to the ball. This method works quite well for the secondary not only because of the distance the ball must travel, but also because the receiver will be in front of the defensive back. It is difficult to see the point of dropping into the middle of a large area and looking at someone standing in front of you to determine what is going on behind you. When the play is a pass, the nature of football rules and the essence of pass protection confine the quarterback to a small area. By design, the quarterback does not want to move from that area (the pocket), and if he does, it is the responsibility of the defensive ends and tackles to keep the quarterback from running the ball. The quarterback is not hard to find. The receivers are the guys who are moving, and if your defenders get close to them, they will find the ball.

At the College of DuPage, when we evaluated the merit of pattern read, the first thing we noticed upon looking at our film was the linebacker's movement in the receiver's zone and how much more quickly the linebackers reacted to the receiver routes. We could see the linebackers cut down or widen their zone as they reacted to the receiver moving through the zones.

Offensive alignment and receiver's routes will change the configuration of your pass zones; thus the size of under coverage zones will depend on the position of the ball and the offensive formation. If the tight end is the widest receiver on one side of an offensive formation, the ball and the tight end are into the hash, with two wide receivers to the open side of the field. The "flat" zone on the tight end side will not be very wide, and the "flat" to the opposite side will be stretched by this formation.

What has been described here is a basic zone coverage concept. We found the same to be true when receivers ran pass routes out of underneath pass zones. Specifically, if the wide receiver on the one-receiver side runs a deep pass route, he in effect eliminates the outside threat to the "flat." Therefore, why should the defense drop to an area of the field if the offense does not have the ability to run a pass route to a zone? As the linebacker makes his drop, getting depth and width, he sees the receiver leave the zone, and he is then free to work back inside. We coined a term, "pulling the shade," as in pulling down a window shade. We would tell our linebackers that when the outside receiver is no longer a threat to the "flat," they should think of the sideline as the top of a window and then "pull the shade" down to the next receiver to the inside (looking for rats). The pattern read will make your linebacker more active on the pass and give the defense more help—and faster help—from the back side of the pass play.

FUNDAMENTALS

We always worked on fundamentals every day: footwork, tackling, getting off blocks, and ball skills. Before starting a drill, we always made sure each player knew the following: what fundamental we were working on, the pace we expected it run at, and how the drill would help improve the skill we were working on. We also kept in mind that every drill has a starting point and a finishing point.

We made the drills competitive and saw that those players not performing the drill were making a mental rep while watching their teammates. We made the fundamental skills a priority, and our athletes knew that the first 15 minutes of every practice would be devoted to fundamental drill work. Every day, we practiced the kicking game. We practiced our punt returns and our blocks for field goals and punts. It was no accident that we won two games—one by using our "all-go" field goal block to block a potential game-winning field goal, and the other by using our all-go punt block to set up a game-winning field goal. Our players had total confidence in their ability to make the blocks, because we practiced them every day. We left nothing to chance. Keep in mind that if you do the little things correctly, then the big things will take care of themselves.

GAME PLAN

Whenever we prepared our game plan at DuPage, we did so without the aid of a computer program that would kick out information about our opponent's tendencies within various formations or its strategy in different down and yardage situations. We believed that the time used in entering data could be put to better use looking at film. The more time we spent looking at film, the better feel we had for how our opponent would attack us. The most important tendency is identifying the opponent's best athletes and how they use them. Therefore, I used a computer program and the printout only to verify what I had already concluded from watching the film. As a coach, you should know your defense and know how to take away what your opponent does best.

The 44 Split defense is designed to stop and contain all offensive plays. Some offensive plays, if run against the 44's base defense, may net positive yards or a first down. Those few plays, including the slant pattern to the strong side or a well-thrown out pattern, will not be a constant source of big yardage. The key is for your players to break on the ball, stop, and contain the play. You should be aware of these plays that work against your base defense and be able to make the necessary adjustment to your defense that will stuff these plays. You should not prepare your team to stop your opponent's entire playbook. Rather, you should prepare your defense to recognize and stop only those plays that are the opponent's most effective plays. Once you have succeeded in this endeavor, you should then prepare to adjust your defense to the flow of the game.

The most important component of your game plan is communication. A great game plan is worthless if you are the only one who understands it. In order to make your game plan work, you must get everyone involved in implementing that game plan—coaches and players. Your game plan should begin taking shape on the Sunday you and your coaches view the game film of your opponent, and it should continue evolving throughout the week of practice. The first thing you should do is gather all the information you have on your upcoming opponent. This information may consist of a game report from a game you have scouted, a film exchange and game film, a scouting report, or a game plan from the previous year. From this information you must determine the following:

- The personnel you will face, including the starting lineup, the backups, the goal line personnel, and the players involved in your opponent's kicking game.

- The substitution of personnel, especially which players come into the game on punts, quick kicks, field goals, fake punts, fake field goals, and special run or pass plays; plus changes in offensive formation and the insertion of any player you need to key in order to tell you the type of play that will be run.

- Any tendencies in formation, personnel, field position, down and distance, and receiver and line splits.

- The matchup of key personnel, the positions of their best players, and the plays used to showcase these standout athletes.

- Their most effective offensive run and pass plays.

- How they will attack you, who you must stop, and what you want to take away from them.

After breaking down the film, you should compile all the information you need for the scouting report that you will give to your players. The scouting report information should be simple to read and contain only those things the players need to know. The scouting report (see sample on pp. 167) is made up mostly of diagrams. It contains formations, backfield sets, offensive plays, the opponent's kicking game, and its goal line offense. The first page contains formation and backfield sets and the jersey numbers of the opposing team's receivers and running backs. At the bottom of the page is a space for covering motion. In addition, space is provided for anything special that needs to be mentioned. The personnel page has your opponent's starting lineup and its backups. The players are listed by position, jersey number, name, height, and weight. Below the lineup is a space for information on the quarterbacks, including their jersey number and whether they are right-handed or left-handed. Also listed by jersey number are the opponent's best running back, best receiver, best lineman, and best offensive player. Information on the opponent's kicking game is listed on this page as well, including which foot the kicker and punter kick with; the names of the holder, the long snapper, and the upback protecting the punter; and the jersey numbers for everyone. Diagrams of the punt, kickoff, and field goal formations are displayed at the bottom of the page.

The next few pages of the scouting report show diagrams of the opponent's run and pass plays. The running plays are listed by "gaps," and each play is named (e.g., ice, base, or power). The passing plays are listed by the action, whether it be three-step drop, seven-step drop, rollout, play-action, or boot pass. The pass routes are given names (arrow, curl, dig, seam, or hitch). These run and pass plays cover only those plays that you will most often see. The opponent's goal line offense is diagrammed on the last page of the scouting report.

The next step is to look at the opponent's offense to see if you need to adjust your base defense. Most of the time, few or no changes to your base defense will be required. Keep in mind that it is always a good idea to first prepare your base defense to play the game. After that, you should look at your opponent's best run and pass plays to see what fronts, stunts, and coverages you will want to run. These adjustments are earmarked for taking advantage of an offensive weakness or helping you in key situations. As an aid, you should list the plays you will see and select the defensive formations, stunts, coverages, or a combination of all three, that you will need to use in order to stop the particular offensive play. When forming this list, you should keep it as simple as possible and throw out any adjustments that may have a chance of causing confusion among your players. The last thing you want is for a player to go into a game unsure of his responsibilities. The adjustments you wish to make must first be discussed among all the coaches, and everyone must be in agreement that the players will be able to comprehend the plan.

Before you go home on Sunday, you should have the game plan and the scouting report prepared for handing out to the players; you should also have the game film of your opponents cut and ready to show to your players. The prepared film of your opponent that is shown to your players is not in a game format. When you show films in a game format, even if it's just the opponent's offensive plays, the players get caught up in the game and don't always see what you would like them to see in the film. Even though it takes a little more time, it is time well spent when you break the film down into a sequence of offensive plays.

At the College of DuPage, the plays we prepared were only those plays we anticipated seeing a lot of and those plays we needed to stop. We started with "A" gap plays, working inside out to "D" gap. The pass plays were at the end of the videotape, which was approximately 20 minutes long. We had the players look at this film before each practice. We felt that when the players saw the different plays in a gap by gap progression, they would concentrate on the play and not on how the game went.

Whenever possible, we liked going into a game with two or three adjustments for each offensive play. Whatever we kept in the game plan depended on our players' ability to grasp and understand the adjustments. Adjustments can be complex or simple. The players' response to our adjustments during the week of practice helped to determine our final game plan. We worked on the game plan throughout the entire week of practice.

Some adjustments we made had to do with the way we would "key" the offense (Our keying system can found in the playbook on p. 65). In a couple of games, one of the offensive players would give us a key we couldn't pass up. In fact, we once played a team that had a balanced attack, with a good running back, two good receivers, and a fine quarterback who could get the ball to them. On Sunday, when we looked at the film of this team, we could see that they had a high-powered offense. We also noticed that this team's entire offensive line would sit back in its stance on pass plays and the linemen would have their weight out over their front hand on run plays. That offensive line was really big, and we had a few mismatches in our defensive front. For that particular game, we made an adjustment to our keys. On each play, we had our defensive ends make a call that would tell the rest of the defense whether the offensive linemen were sitting back in their stances or keeping their weight out over their hands. If the ends made a "birds" call, that meant the offensive linemen were sitting back in their stances and preparing for a pass play. If the ends made a "pigs" call, that meant the offensive linemen were leaning forward in preparation for a running play. We called a combination of two fronts, stunts, and coverages in the defensive huddle—one for run ("pigs") and one for pass ("birds"). The defensive call sounded something like this: "Pigs, 60 cover 3, Mike and Meg read—birds, stack cover 5." We would run the front, stunt, or coverage according to whatever the call was—"birds" or "pigs." Their offense never had a chance. We were always in the correct defense.

The players really got into using the "birds" and "pigs" call, and we had such great results that this system became something we looked forward to implementing against every opponent. We had two ends who got so good at making these calls that they could even tell each other which side the trap block was coming from. (With "pigs" on one side and "birds" on the other side, the trap block was coming from the "birds" side.)

GAME WEEK AND PRACTICE

At DuPage, during our week of practice, the players worked on the techniques they needed to learn so that they could make the necessary adjustments for that Saturday's opponent. They also worked on our overall game plan during individual, group, and team time. At Monday's practice, half the time was spent in the classroom. The previous game's film was viewed by the players, while the coaches highlighted both proper and unacceptable play. The scouting report and the game plan were passed out to the players. The last half of Monday's practice was spent on the field, where we would walk through our opponent's offense, as well as our game plan.

Before practice on Tuesday, the players watched the prepared film of our opponent. The players were required to come to the film room already dressed and taped, and from there they would go out onto the practice field. Our prework time was a 15-minute period that preceded the time blocked out for stretching exercises. We usually devoted our prework time to improving such skills as communication and alignment. Consequently, we liked to run a drill called " Flash Cards." This drill involved the use of five rubber welcome mats representing offensive linemen and line splits. At the outset of the drill, the coach would hold up a flash card displaying a diagram of the opponent's offensive formation and backfield set to the second group of offensive linebackers and secondary players. The players in the second group would then respond by breaking from the huddle and aligning themselves on the rubber mats, as receivers and offensive backs in the offensive formation reflected on the flash card. Our base defense served as the alignment, and the defensive team would line up quickly, making all the proper calls. After a quick check by the coaches, we were ready for the next offensive formation. We usually got through three sets of 10 formations. We worked on every type of formation that we might see; that way, there would be no surprises.

If our game plan involved any read technique or alignment movement, we would work on those first at the individual level; then at the unit level; and, finally, at the team level. During team time, our "scout team" (as mentioned earlier, our second-team defensive unit) would wear each opponent's jersey number. When the scout team wore those jerseys, the players could more clearly see the other team's substitution patterns, their use of personnel, and how all that movement fit into their offense.

It was very important to us that all the players understood the role of this scout team and what we needed to accomplish during team time. Our players knew that in order to be prepared for our opponent, we must have our scout team resemble that opponent as closely as possible. During film, the coaches helped that cause by pointing out tendencies that we needed to see from our scout team.

During team time on Tuesday, we stayed in our base defense and tried to get 15 plays with our first unit and 10 with the second unit. Running team time with defensive players is more productive than using offensive players for a scout team. The players on the scout team have a vested interest in what they are doing and, as a result, are determined to prepare for the game. When they run the offensive plays, the scout team is also learning our opponent's offense. Also, when the first unit takes the place of the second unit on the scout team, it presents an opportunity to see the opponent from the offensive side of the ball.

Wednesday's and Thursday's practices were the same as Tuesday's, but, with the exception of team time, we added the fronts, stunts, and coverages to the team-time script. Also, we worked on the passing game during group time. We walked through and ran the opponent's pass plays against our different coverages. (For all of our man-to-man coverage defenses, Nickel Dog and Prevent Dog and 65 Dog, we used the same alignment and assignment for the under coverage. Whenever possible, we kept the same personnel; that way, when we worked on one coverage, we were also working on all of the man-to-man coverages.)

On Wednesday and Thursday we had team time for our goal line unit. On Wednesday the coaches would make the decision on what is in and what is out of the game plan. Friday's practice was short, and we had an extended team time. During team time, we matched the offensive plays to the defensive adjustment we would possibly counter with in the game. After team time on Friday, we came together as a team to go through "sudden change." In sudden change, all the players got together on the sideline and Coach MacDougall called out to the middle of the field, one by one, all special teams, both offense and defense. The coaches would take this opportunity to check to see if everything was all set as the different teams came onto the field and huddled.

In addition, the offensive and defensive teams would meet in their classrooms to take a short, written test on the game plan and scouting report. By the end of practice on Friday, the coaches and players were well prepared for our opponent.

GAME-WEEK PRACTICE DAY (TUESDAY THROUGH THURSDAY)

2:00—TREATMENT AND TAPING

2:45—FILMS (20 minutes)

Come to classroom ready to go to the practice field.

3:15—PREWORK (15 minutes)

3:30—TEAM STRETCHING AND FORM RUNNING (10 minutes)

3:40—THUD (5 minutes)

Offensive running plays against the defense from the 20-yard line going in. Live blocking, and the backs are not tackled. Offense and defense is scripted.

3:45—INDIVIDUAL PERIOD (15 minutes)

Work on fundamentals.

4:00—UNIT WORK (15 minutes)

Working as individual defensive units (front, linebackers, and secondary).

4:15—GROUP WORK (20 minutes)

Linebackers and secondary 7-on-7 vs. offensive; tackles and ends 1-on-1; and unit pass rush vs. offense.

4:35—PUNT WORK (15 minutes)

Punt returns and blocks vs. offense.

4:50—TEAM TIME (25 minutes)

Opponent's plays.

5:15—KICKING GAME (10 minutes)

Field goal blocks and kickoff vs. offense.

5:25—SPRINTS (10 minutes)

Run in offensive and defensive units: 1. All offensive and defensive linemen. 2. Linebackers, tight ends, and fullbacks. 3. Tailbacks, quarterbacks, and secondary.

GAME AND PRESS BOX MANAGEMENT

On game day, all the preparation and work you have done during the week can go down the drain, if you're not organized. Decisions must be made quickly, you can not hesitate, and time is your enemy. You must be able to see the complete picture and also see through the eyes of your coaches and players. Many a good coach has lost it on game day because of an inability to get a clear picture of what is happening on the field. On Sunday, when you look at the game video, you don't have to be a genius to see where things went wrong. The secret is to have "Sunday Vision" on Saturday. Preparation, organization, and communication are the keys to staying one step in front of your opponent.

When you have had a good week of practice, your team is prepared for your opponent. The worst thing you can do—on the heels of all this preparation—is to blow it all by not being prepared to control the play and the management of the game. As a coach, you face four areas of concern: (1) your sideline and personnel, (2) game substitutions and special teams, (3) press box management, and (4) game adjustments. Your sideline must be a working area—not a box seat for spectators. (I always told our players that if they want to watch the game, they should buy a ticket.) The sideline is for athletes who are playing a football game, and they need to concentrate on the game at all times. If you were facing the College of DuPage sideline, you would see all the defensive players well to the right side of the 50-yard line. Everyone has a task to perform, and they must focus on doing their job. Those players who are in backup roles must understand that they are only one play away from being a starter. Those who are not playing in the game should be helping their teammates who are playing and preparing themselves for when they get into the game. We would tell our players on the sideline to watch their particular position on the field and the opponent's play. They should see how their position is being played and whether the opponent is showing any tendencies. The backup players should also take the time to discuss the play of the opponent with the starter.

Those personnel who are involved in special teams must be prepared to go into the game a down before they know they will need to. They must know the jersey numbers of those opponents who will key what special team goes into the game. These special teams players need to follow the play of the game and anticipate their going into the game. Your special teams coach is usually your defensive front coach. The special teams coach and players must be on the same page or a step ahead of the defensive coordinator. The special teams will report to the special teams coach (who has a depth chart of all the different special teams) before going onto the field.

It was my policy at DuPage that during the game, these teams, as they are called by the special teams coach, must stand behind me on the sideline. The special teams players were the only defensive players I would allow across the offensive side of the 50-yard line. As you well know, there are points in the game where you must be able to send into the game one of these special teams, depending on what your opponent elects to do. I can recall a game where we used four different special teams and defenses on four consecutive downs.

The depth charts for all special teams and defenses were posted on the defensive team's bulletin board every Tuesday. During the game week, we practiced the "sudden change" substitution with our special teams and defense. We did this during team time by putting a special team play in the script at different points. We worked on sudden change during our two-minute drill, which is run against the offense and simulates the action that would take place with two minutes left in the game. Our kicking game periods were devoted to special teams, and sudden change was the last thing we did on the field at Friday's practice.

If any player has an equipment problem or is injured, it is the responsibility of the player and his backup to notify the coaches. The substitutions resulting from these equipment problems or injuries can be a disaster, if the backup player is not prepared to go into the game. As soon as we felt we had the game in hand, we started to substitute our backup players. In fact, we tried to get our backups into the game as soon as possible. For the backup player to be able to go into a game in a key situation and perform as a starter, he will need game experience. For their part, the players who are coming out of the game are to keep their gear on and their minds on the game; it is now their job to help the backup players who have replaced them on the field. Keep in mind that when substitutions are made, it is important that the area coaches have most of the input regarding who is the starter and who is to be substituted into the game. You must give these coaches the responsibility to make those decisions, and they must be willing to take on the responsibility. Although the final decision is the coordinator's, he should make it on Sunday, and not on game day.

When the players came off the field after an opponent's offensive series, the first thing we would do, before anything else, was to have the players be seated on the bench at the far right of the defensive sideline. We had a seating chart, and the front four players sat on the ground in front of the bench, with the ends on the outside and the tackles in the middle. The linebackers sat on the bench, and the inside linebackers sat in the middle. The secondary stood behind the others, with the safety in the middle. The remaining defensive players gathered around those who had just come off the field. At this point the coaches would talk to them about their play and their adjustments and go through the opponent's series play by play. During this time, the defense's play was evaluated by the field coaches, the coach in the press box, and the players themselves. This information must be gathered quickly, clearly, and from all available sources. The players will be one of your best sources, provided you have supplied them with a means of communicating that is fast and simple. You must then decipher from this information what needs to be done to alter the success of your opponent. You need to know what is going on out there; you don't need coaches and players yelling out solutions, adjustments, stunts, or coverages to you. If there is a problem, you should find out what that problem is and then fix it. You will be successful in this endeavor if the information you receive from the press box is understandable, clear, and presented to you in a prearranged, orderly manner. If you are not getting information this way, then you are to blame.

A coaching friend once asked me to work the press box for him during his game, because he was having problems getting the type of information he needed to help him make adjustments. When I got to the press box, I saw six coaches and two sets of headphones. During the entire game, all I did was observe what went on. The game was a high school game, and the three defensive coaches working the press box were a varsity assistant and a freshman and a sophomore coach. What I saw was that the information that was going down to the field was ineffective and confusing. "This player is killing us," "The referee made a real bad call," "We need to run Cover I." These were the types of things I was hearing called down to the field by anyone who could get the field coach's attention. After the game, my friend told me he was not going to let the under-level coaches in the press box anymore, because they were causing confusion. I told him he was to blame for the confusion because he hadn't given those coaches instruction on the information he needed. Actually, nothing is wrong with having twice the number of people in the press box as my friend had—as long as you give each of them a specific job to do.

Your information from the press box must be as clear to you as if you were sitting in the film room watching a video of the play. You need to tell your coaches what you need to hear so that you are able to see the play.

At DuPage, I had a set order of information that the coach in the press box would relay to me before, during, and after the play. The first bit of information I needed to hear was the position of the ball, the yard line, and the hash. Next, I wanted to know the down and the distance, followed by the specifics of the offense's formation, its backfield set, and a description of the play. When referring to the play, the viewpoint would be from the offensive side of the ball. Right and left would become top and bottom, as I looked at the field from the sideline. The area of the play would be relayed by strong or weak gaps. The final thing I wanted to hear was the gain and a short comment, if necessary. The following commentary is an example of what I would hear from a coach in the press box: "Ball on the 25, hash at the bottom, 1st and 10, blue split to the top, tear strong, the tackle got reached." This message was what I needed to hear in order to see the play in my mind. Language is very important when someone is trying to describe a play to you quickly.

The press box coaches look for formation and substitution patterns, and they also chart the offense. With their help, we are better able to pick up and verify tendencies. Furthermore, on the basis of who the opponent is substituting into the game, the coaches in the press box can tell the coordinator on the field what the offensive formation is going to be—before the offensive team is even in its huddle.

At DuPage, we charted the offensive running and passing attack during the game. The run chart is really simple and easy to keep: The jersey number of the back who carried the ball is written in a space that breaks down the running play by strongside and weakside gaps. The pass chart is also simple. We referred to it as the "shot chart," because it was borrowed from the basketball coaches. Our shot chart was a diagram of our passing zones, with space provided below the chart to write in the type of pass play that was used. When a pass was thrown to a receiver, the jersey number of the receiver was recorded at the approximate point in the zone on the chart. The jersey number was circled if the receiver caught the pass. From these charts, we were able to get a series-by-series tendency of the strongside and weakside gap running plays, which ball carrier was running to which gap, and where the quarterback likes to throw and to which receiver.

Before each game, I would diagram our opponent's top six or seven running plays and pass plays. I then made two copies of this list, with the pass plays noted on one side and the run plays on the other, and each play was numbered. I called this our "quick list," which I would later refer to during a game, whenever I needed to verify or discuss an offensive play by our opponent with the press box coach. Instead of a lengthy description of a blocking scheme or a pass route, the coach in the press box could simply tell me the number of the play on our "quick list." Thanks to this means of communication, I could now see the game from two vantage points. What the offense was doing to attack our defense was no longer a guessing game, and we were learning to take advantage of all our resources and everybody on our staff.

We got to the point where our players would come off the field and give the coaches a clear picture of what went on during the previous series of offensive plays. The players were able to verify the type of play that was run and understand how it was being blocked. They also knew what gap the play hit and who carried the ball or who ran what type of pass route. The communication between the sideline coaches, the press box, and the players will give you a clear picture of what is happening. When the offense was having success in moving the ball, the adjustments we used were always the simplest and most effective. The adjustments were based on the information we received and were prepared counters to an attack at the gap, blocking schemes, or pass plays. The players realized their input was important and were honored that they were asked about their play. They understood that it is important to know how the offense is attacking you.

The players were more confident, because they saw the same jersey numbers, line splits, formations, sets, and offensive plays that they had practiced against during the week. The players and coaches soon believed they could stop anything the offense might throw at us, because we could see it, and we were already prepared for it.

CHAPTER 5

Footwork, Tackling, Trapping the Ball, and Interception Drills

Too often, we as coaches make judgments about youngsters and say things like "The kid can't tackle," while at the same, we have neglected to teach him how to tackle. Your team can become better at tackling, but it must be taught from the ground up—and from start to finish.

Every time I either think or talk about teaching tackling, I'm always reminded of this one particular player we had at the College of DuPage. This kid was one of those undersized overachievers who was not a great athlete but who somehow managed to beat great athletes. He played a weak outside linebacker, a position that calls for a good open-field tackler. As a freshman, Tim could not make a tackle; as a result, he did not get much playing time. The next season, when Tim was a sophomore, we found that we were four deep at his position. Because he was the only sophomore at his position, he was running with the first group about the time we started practice. I recall telling the other defensive coaches that it was going to be a long year if we had to start Tim at the Sara linebacker position. After our first scrimmage, I moved Tim to the fourth unit because his tackling hadn't shown any signs of improvement. After practice, Tim asked if he could talk with me. He wanted to know what he had to do to get his starting job back. I told Tim the other three players were bigger and faster than he was. Although they needed to improve their tackling, I was going to give them a look. I told Tim that in order for him to move up on the depth chart, he had to become a better tackler. The next few weeks, that kid drove me nuts. When we ran a drill, he would be the first in line. During those drills, if everyone would get two repetitions, Tim would somehow get four. If I would correct Tim on his technique, he would go back to the front of the line and do it again. I would see him working before and after practice on a certain skill with which he was having problems. Through hard work, Tim improved his tackling and once again became our starting Sara linebacker—just in time for our season opener. The Sunday before our fourth game, at our coaches' meeting, I recall one of the coaches saying, "If Tim gets hurt, we are in trouble." When we reached mid-season, not only was Tim making open-field tackles, but he was also knocking the ball carrier on his back.

In our last game of the regular season, we were playing a team that had a wide receiver who was an All-American as a freshman. This athlete was also having a great sophomore year and was leading the nation in kickoff and punt returns. Undoubtedly, he would repeat as an All-American. Going into the game, our team and his were both 9-0. Because of the way their team aligned, Tim was responsible for the flat to the side of this standout receiver. Their quarterback tried to get the ball into the hands of this receiver with hitch routes, flanker screens, and slants. We wound up winning the game, 31-6, and this All-American managed only six catches for 15 yards.

Now, Tim was not a great athlete, nor was he fast. He was just determined to do it right and was able to humble a great athlete. The moral of the story is that any player can be taught to be a good tackler.

The most important thing I've learned in my 30 years of coaching, including 23 years as the defensive coordinator at the College of DuPage, is that your team can and must be taught how to tackle as a team. Tackling must be taught from the ground up. It also must be taught on three levels—individual, unit, and team. When your defense is attacking the ball carrier with a team plan and working together to take away all of the ball carrier's options by the angles of approach, you're making it an eleven-on-one game: everybody is after the guy with the ball.

After reading and listening to most of what has been written or said about tackling, I've come to the conclusion that there is some kind of conspiracy going on in defensive football. The origin of this conspiracy lies in the fact that most defensive coaches, myself included, are old, frustrated offensive linemen. My basis for this presumption is the similarities between how offensive linemen are taught to move and what is considered good tackling form. As coaches, we need to think about what exactly we consider "proper" form and what our athletes are able to do physically. What is sometimes considered proper technique can actually be a contradiction of body mechanics. Take, for example, the following description, which is generally considered excellent advice for tacklers: Keep feet shoulder-width apart, take short steps, drive through the ball carrier, put your helmet on the football, keep your head up, and wrap up the ball carrier with your arms. If you look closely at this statement, and then think about what a tackler actually must do in order to take down a ball carrier, I'm sure you will find flaws in this tackling technique. I've looked at a lot of film, and the only time I've seen a player make a tackle from a position of "feet shoulder-width apart" has been when the back has run over the top of the tackler or there was no place for the back to go. Under no circumstances can a tackler close at full speed to the ball carrier and come to a balanced position with his "feet shoulder-width apart" just before making contact with the ball carrier. For a tackler running at full speed to assume a balanced position with his feet that distance apart, he must first come to a complete stop— and with his weight on his heels. For the tackler to then redirect to the ball carrier, he must do so while stationary, and while keeping his weight on his heels.

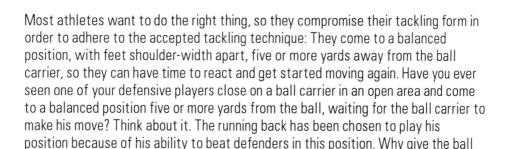

Most athletes want to do the right thing, so they compromise their tackling form in order to adhere to the accepted tackling technique: They come to a balanced position, with feet shoulder-width apart, five or more yards away from the ball carrier, so they can have time to react and get started moving again. Have you ever seen one of your defensive players close on a ball carrier in an open area and come to a balanced position five or more yards from the ball, waiting for the ball carrier to make his move? Think about it. The running back has been chosen to play his position because of his ability to beat defenders in this position. Why give the ball carrier the opportunity to make the first move?

At the College of DuPage, we told our players that if we see them breaking down five yards from the ball carrier, they are coming out of the game. We also told them that as long as they are forcing the ball carrier to redirect, the missed tackle is not a complete loss. When the tackler is coming hard on a good angle, the missed tackle is going to force the ball carrier into someone else (eleven against one). The proper way to teach your tacklers is to instruct them to always close to the ball at full speed on one of three angles—the outside shoulder, head-up, or the back hip of the ball carrier. Which one of these aim points the tackler will use depends on his angle of approach and the path the ball carrier takes. The tackler must adjust his angle on the ball carrier as the run develops. His aim point, for example, can change from back hip to outside shoulder.

When a tackler takes an aim point, he takes away the ball carrier's options and forces him to make a decision, usually before the runner would like to. Just before he makes contact with the ball carrier, the tackler idles down with his feet under his hips and then drops his hips as if he is going to jump. The analogy we liked to use with our players is of a wide receiver making a pass route cut who idles down by bringing his feet together and dropping his hips. When the receiver redirects, his first step is a power step, and his body weight is shifted forward. The tackler therefore should take a path, at full speed, to the ball carrier, which will force him to either run into the tackler or change his direction. When the tackler reaches the idle-down point (within two yards of the ball carrier), the tackler should drop his hips, squeeze his knees together, and stagger his feet. At this point, the tackler should either explode into the ball carrier or redirect to the ball carrier with power and speed. Using this tackling form, the tackler can react quickly and powerfully. He has also reduced the number of options for the ball carrier, who must either run into the tackler or redirect in the direction the tackler is forcing him in order to avoid the tackler.

We emphasized this type of footwork for tackling and taking on blocks in the open. Our footwork drills worked on teaching the athlete the proper footwork used in tackling, idling down, and stepping into the ball carrier. When we drilled on our footwork, we told our players to "squeeze knees, drop the hips, and get little feet" (i.e., keep your feet together and use short steps). We used tackling and trap-the-ball drills designed to work on closing to the ball carrier, taking the proper angle, getting to the idle-down point, redirecting, and using the proper contact technique. Every day, we worked on these skills in an individual or combined situation, depending on which drill we used.

I also find fault with what is considered good technique for a tackler to use upon impact with the ball carrier. When you tell a tackler to put his helmet on the ball and wrap up with his arms, it brings to mind a swimmer diving into a pool. After all, when a defender strikes the ball carrier or takes on an offensive blocker, he uses similar body mechanics. Once again, when we work on one technique, we are working on both.

We used to tell our players that when they tackle a ball carrier, their upper-body movement should resemble a two-handed punch, with their elbows pointing down. The front part of their shoulder pad should make contact between the ball carrier's numbers. The tackler's helmet should come low to high and then up and under the ball carrier's shoulder pad to the ball side. The tackler should then punch through with his arms and grab the back of the opponent's jersey with his hands (i.e., grab cloth). If the ball carrier's number is 27, the tackler should have the big 2 in his left hand and the big 7 in his right. Next, the tackler should run through the ball carrier, using short steps. One of the biggest problems athletes have is keeping their head up while getting under the ball carrier's pads. We don't want them to knock the ball carrier backwards. All we need them to do is pop the ball carrier up and drive him backwards.

We always told our players that it should be easy for them to grasp the concept of making the ball carrier "pop up." All they have to do is understand that it is leverage—not force or strength—that accomplishes that goal. We would use the following analogy to point out how simple it is to get the ball carrier to pop up: If you try to pick up a 45-pound plate that's lying face down on the floor, you will encounter great difficulty getting your fingers underneath it to grip it and lift it up. Once you manage to get your fingers underneath it, you can pop it up with only two fingers. The key to lifting the plate is to get under the surface so you can take advantage of leverage.

The point is that without leverage, force and strength are not factors. Therefore, if the tackler is going to be successful, he must strike the ball carrier on a line that runs under the ball carrier's shoulder pads and travels up and through him. In order to gain the advantage, the tackler must drop his hips, using a front-foot–to–back-foot stagger, squeeze his knees, and get little feet. Once his helmet level is below the ball carrier's shoulder pads, the tackler can then use his own shoulder pads to "pop up" the ball carrier. If the tackler strikes the ball carrier between the numbers, goes under and up through the runner's shoulder pads, and moves low to high, he will drive the ball carrier backwards. Ball carriers don't run low to the ground all the time; like the tackler, they must lower their body on contact—but they do so by bending at the waist. Because he bends at his hips and knees, the tackler will generate more striking power than the ball carrier. In this scenario, the low man wins.

If you want to make sure your tackler is always the low man, you must drill him on the proper technique, teaching him through a progression that begins with footwork and ends with trapping the ball as a team.

FOOTWORK DRILLS

In this first footwork drill, the player should step over the top of each bag, keeping his feet together and both feet down before moving on to the next bag. Keeping his hips down, his shoulders over his hips, and his feet under his hips, the player should refrain from hopping.

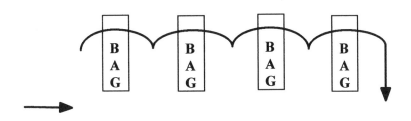

In this drill, the player should sidestep and shuffle, keeping his feet together. He should explode up to midpoint and back out, keeping his feet tight. He should also keep his hips down, his shoulders over his hips, and his feet under his hips.

Again, keeping his feet together, the player should sidestep and shuffle. He should then explode up to midpoint and shuffle across and back out, keeping his feet tight. The player should make sure to keep his hips down, his shoulders over his hips, and his feet under his hips.

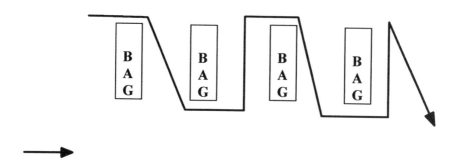

The player begins this drill from the prone position, lying face down in the middle hole between the bags. On command from the coach, the player should pop up and sidestep over the bags, getting both of his feet down in the hole. Upon reaching the end, the player should move back through the bags in the opposite direction. After stepping over the last bag, he should sprint up to the coach and, on the coach's signal, redirect to the cone.

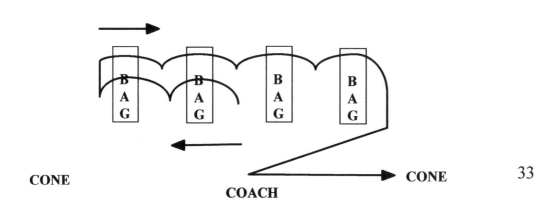

33

TACKLING DRILLS

Hips Up
The ball carrier and the tackler lie on their backs, helmet to helmet, one yard apart, between the cones. On the coach's command of "hit," the tackler and the ball carrier should roll toward the same cone while getting to their feet. On contact, they should work to get their feet under their hips. The player who is able to get his feet under his hips first should drive the other player backwards. This drill provides the coach with an effective way to teach players how to keep their feet moving after contact.

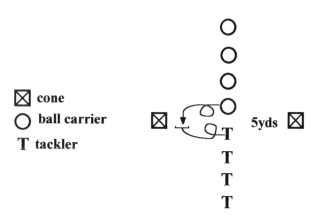

Wake-up

The ball carrier and the tackler set up by facing each other inside the five-yard triangle. The ball carrier is positioned in front of one cone, and the tackler is positioned between the other two cones. On the coach's command of "hit," the ball carrier should run toward the inside edge of one of the two cones in front of him. The ball carrier should be sure to give the tackler a low target. On the movement of the ball carrier, the tackler should attack the ball carrier, driving for his outside shoulder. (The tackler should use the technique that was covered earlier in this chapter.) The tackler should drive hard off of his outside foot and square his hips to the ball carrier. The tackler should not put the ball carrier down.

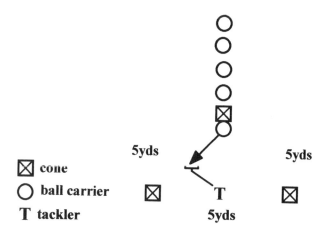

Lateral Bump

On the coach's command of "hit," the ball carrier should run at the tackler. Using the proper technique, the tackler should bump and punch the ball carrier, keeping his helmet to the outside. After contact, the tackler should release the ball carrier and give ground while moving down the line toward the cone to the outside. The ball carrier, once he is released, should spin off the tackler, back and to the outside. The ball carrier and tackler should square up and repeat the tackle. After the second tackle, the ball carrier should spin in the opposite direction for two more tackles, and the tackler should attack the opposite shoulder of the ball carrier.

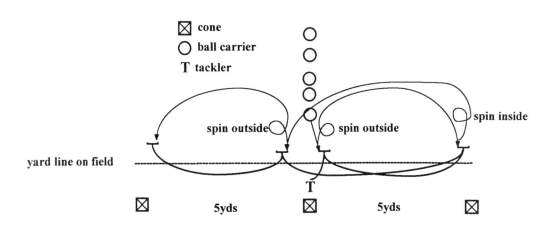

TACKLING DRILLS

The following three tackling drills are designed to teach players how to use the proper technique when closing to and redirecting to the ball carrier. While participating in these drills, players should keep in mind the three most common errors made by tacklers: (1) not closing to the ball carrier at full speed; (2) idling down to redirect while too far away from the ball carrier; and (3) placing their feet too far apart in a balanced position and thus causing their first step on redirection to be short and off balance.

#1: The tackler should run at full speed to the cone. In order to redirect, he should squeeze his knees together and drop his hips, keeping his weight on the balls of his feet. This maneuver will enable him to take a power step when redirecting. On the coach's movement, the tackler should redirect to the cone.

#2: One tackler from each of the two lines of tacklers should run at full speed to the cone, idle down just before he reaches the cone, and then redirect to the next cone. Watch for mistakes in the tacklers' technique, making sure that they are at full speed—not idling down too soon or getting their feet too far apart. The tacklers should race each other to the cones.

#3: The ball carrier should sprint to the cone directly in front of him and then break to the cone to his right. The tackler should run the drill as before, but redirect to the ball carrier. When the tackler reaches the ball carrier, the tackler should extend his hands up and into the pads of the ball carrier, keeping the ball carrier at arm's length.

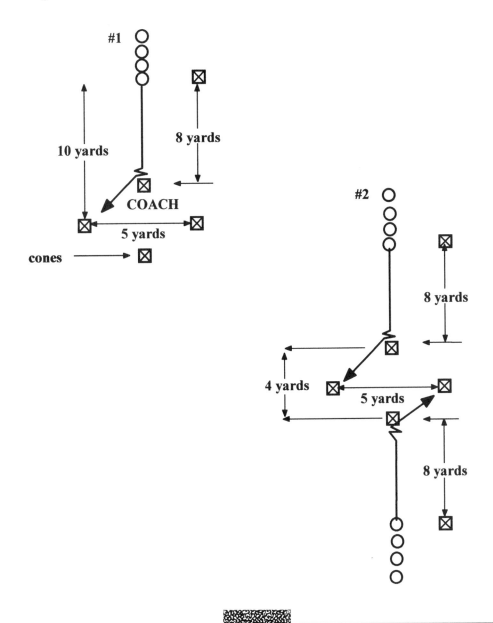

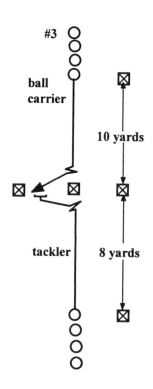

#3

ball carrier

10 yards

tackler   8 yards

TRAPPING THE BALL

Often, when coaches tell their players that they need great pursuit to the football, they are teaching them the last-resort method to get to the football. The word "pursuit" is defined in the dictionary (in part) as "follow[ing] in an effort to overtake and chase ..." According to this definition, a defensive team that has great pursuit is chasing ball carriers into the end zone. Actually, the opposite is true. Rather than teach pursuit, you should be teaching your players to trap and contain the ball carrier.

The first step for the tackler should be to take a direct angle to the ball carrier and then close that angle at full speed. The angle should be aimed at one of three points, which will depend on the tackler's approach angle to the ball: the ball carrier's outside shoulder, head-up, or the ball carrier's back hip. The tackler should close quickly on the ball carrier, forcing him to either run into the tackler or redirect. When you think about it, a ball carrier has only three options: straight, right, or left. The tackler should not give the ball carrier an opportunity to work on the tackler. Instead, the tackler should force the ball carrier to react to the tackler. Therefore, the tackler should take an angle that will take away two of the ball carrier's options. When closing from the outside, the tackler should run at the outside shoulder of the ball carrier, limiting the runner's choice to the inside. If one of the tackler's teammates takes the same approach, the ball carrier will be trapped and contained. Defensive players should keep in mind that if they work together, they can take away all of the ball carrier's options by using the proper angle of approach. On defense, it's eleven against one—everyone is after the guy with the ball! These drills will teach players how to trap the ball carrier. However, it is important throughout the drills for coaches to remind their players to employ the tackling technique they learned from the tackling drills.

The ball carrier should run forward at full speed and make a cut to either the right or the left. The tackler should close on the ball carrier at full speed, taking an outside-shoulder-approach angle. When the ball carrier makes his cut, the tackler should adjust as he closes. When the tackler reaches the ball carrier, he should extend his hands up into the pads of the ball carrier, keeping him at arm's length.

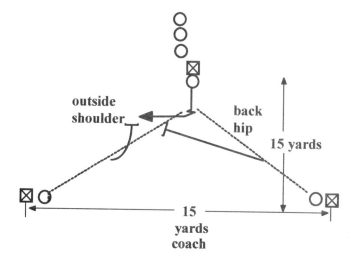

On the command of the coach, all of the tacklers should make a pass drop. (Defensive linemen should do a hip row in the direction the coach points.) The coach will hand the ball to the back, who should then either break to the outside or go outside and cut back inside. The tacklers should work together, using good angles to trap the ball.

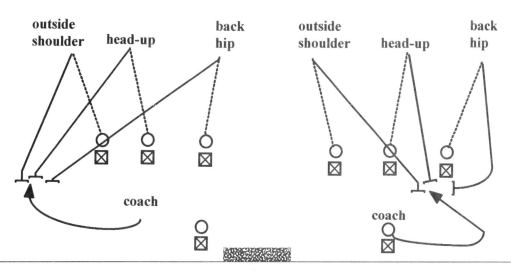

TRAP-THE-BALL DRILLS

These drills involve the same skills and techniques that were discussed in the section on tackling drills. The drills are run on one side and then the other. At the start of the drills, the coach will signal the snap, and everyone will make a pass drop. The coach will hand the ball to the ball carrier, who should be breaking outside or cutting back. The secondary and the linebackers should break up on the ball carrier, using the proper technique and angles. The secondary and the linebackers must work together (outside shoulder, head-up, and back hip). The coach should also run the drill with one position running a stunt.

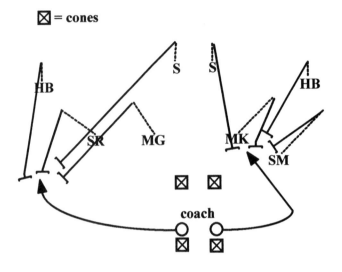

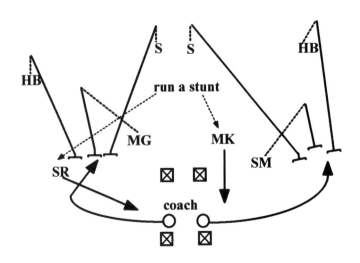

This drill is the same as the previous drill, except that it also works on the back-side angles. The defense can also run stunts from this drill.

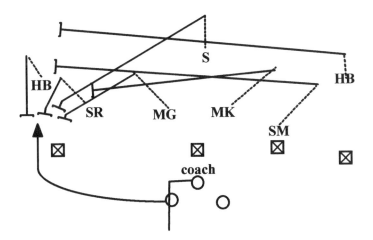

These drills can be run with the tackles and the ends. The front-side tackle and the end should rush pass to the cone and then trap the ball from the back side. The back-side tackle and the end should take two steps toward the ball. The tackle should close to the ball down the line of scrimmage. The back-side end ensures that the ball crosses the line of scrimmage and then takes a cutoff angle to the ball.

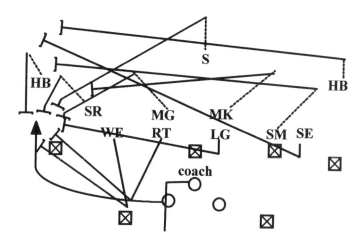

TEAM TRAP-THE-BALL

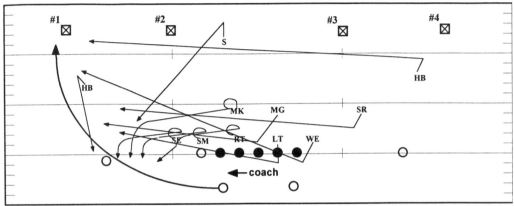

● = Rubber door mats for offensive linemen and line splits.

☒ = cones

The primary purpose of this drill is to teach the fundamentals of trapping the ball carrier as a team. The coaches should be assigned to specific player positions so they can check for alignment and angles to the ball carrier. Once the players have an understanding of the drill, the coaches can incorporate other teaching into the drill, including alignment, assignment, stunts, and adjustments.

The setup for the drill includes five rubber doormats which represent the offensive linemen and their splits. Four cones are placed 12 yards from the ball on the numbers and hashes. The "scout team" will be made up of the second-unit linebackers and secondary. The coach will bring the scout team together in a huddle, where he will tell the players the backfield set, the formation, the direction of the ball carrier, and the cone they should run to. After the scout team breaks from the huddle and aligns on the ball, the coaches will make a quick check of the defense to ensure proper alignment. The coach will step in the direction the ball is going and hand off the ball to the ball carrier. The ball carrier should always break to the outside of the defensive formation and run to the assigned cone. The ball carrier should be running at three-quarters speed and then increase his speed as the defensive players become accustomed to the drill. On the movement of the coach and the players' key, the defense should react to the play. The defensive front (the ends, the tackles, and the linebackers) to the ball carrier's side seat-rolls and "buzzes the ball." When we tell our players to "buzz the ball," we want them to close hard to the ball carrier on a proper angle so that they come close to him without actually touching him. The front to the back side of the play should attack the line of scrimmage (no seat-roll).

The end and the tackle should cross the line of scrimmage, collect, and then close hard to the ball on a good angle. The two linebackers should attack the line of scrimmage, collect, and then close hard to the ball on a good angle. On the coach's movement, the secondary should take its three-step drop and react to the ball carrier, closing hard to the ball on a good angle.

RETURNS, INTERCEPTIONS, FUMBLES, AND BLOCKED KICKS

The defense has four opportunities on which to score: (1) an interception, (2) a fumble, (3) a blocked kick or punt, and (4) a punt return. It has been said that close games are determined by the kicking game and field position. Certainly, the defense wants to make good on every chance to score, or at least to put its own offense in a position to score. When an opportunity to score occurs, we will set a "wall" return to the closest sideline. The reason we want to set our wall to the closest sideline is that after every down, the ball is placed somewhere between the hashes, making this area the site of the biggest concentration of offensive players. When the offensive team becomes the defensive team during a play, it has to fan out and cover the field. On our wall returns, we want to set the wall quickly and to the point farthest away from the concentration of offensive players. On turnovers, fumbles, interceptions, and blocked kicks, we will set the wall on the fly. We will make a "bingo" call to the closest sideline, "Bingo left." Everybody should get to the numbers of the side of the "bingo" call and set a wall. After making the "bingo" call, the returner must get to the wall, even if he has to give ground to do so. Once the returner is at the wall, he should turn it upfield, staying about a yard in bounds. Players should keep in mind that when blocking on a return, they cannot block below the waist or from behind. Sometimes a "no block" is better than an attempt that goes wrong.

INTERCEPTION DRILL

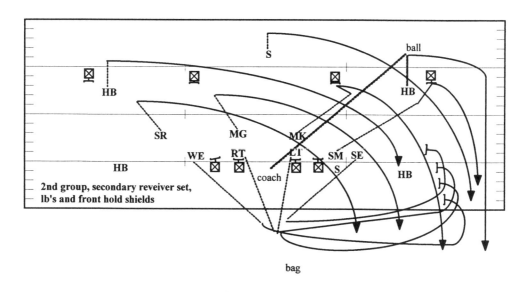

bag

The coach begins the drill by signaling for the snap. At that point, the secondary and the linebackers make a pass drop. The front should make a pass-rush move on a player holding a shield and rush to an upright bag or a cone. The coach will then throw the ball to one of the linebackers or a player from the secondary. Whoever makes the interception should make the "bingo" call to the nearest sideline and then run the return up the sideline. The linebackers and the secondary should take the nearest receiver off the ball (i.e., the player holding the shield) and lead upfield. The back-side linebackers and the secondary should get across and upfield. The front should form a wall on the numbers to the side of the "bingo" call (the nearest sideline). The primary coaching point is to always check that the players understand alignment and assignment.

CHAPTER 6

Read Drills

During my first few years at the College of DuPage, I emulated most coaches by using drills that would isolate certain skills and techniques. When we ran drills that were designed to improve game-day performance, I expected my players to display a game-like intensity.

Our read drills became a game, and the players and the coaches were always looking for a winner. Read drills became like scrimmage, and if the drills didn't reach the desired intensity, the coaches would reprimand players. As we soon discovered, we were working on winning drills and not on learning how to win. In other words, we were not teaching our defensive players to respond to the offense's movement. My mistake was confusing a player's emotional and physical response to a drill with teaching a player how to respond to a game situation.

Defensive football is a game of reaction to an offensive stimulus. Reaction must be taught through repetition. After a time, athletes will quickly and appropriately react, as they become more familiar with the stimulus through repetition. When we realized our mistake, we changed our approach to practice and drills. We made it a point to never leave the player in the dark on what we were trying to accomplish by doing the drill. Before each drill, the coach went through the purpose, the pace, and the expected outcome of the drill. When we decided to teach a certain skill, we sought to identify and isolate that particular skill or technique. We used a drill which isolated and repeated that skill. Once the skill was mastered, we expanded on and developed the drills to incorporate other skills.

The purpose of read drills is to teach speed in reacting to movement, as well as recognition of offensive schemes that enables the defensive players to locate the ball. We are not working on getting off blocks or tackling the ball carrier. The drills start out simple by isolating small segments of the total play. The drills are limited to just a few offensive plays, and these plays are given a name. When possible, neither a ball nor a quarterback is used during the drills. Those two omissions enable the defensive player to recognize the offensive play by the movement of keys, the backfield action, and the blocking schemes. More offensive players and plays are added to the drill as the defense progresses. The following drills show how we teach our players to read and react.

TACKLES AND ENDS 3-ON-2 DRILLS

This drill is one of the most effective read drills for the defensive front. The coach can run the drill in many different ways. It is quick and easy to set up. Two groups can be run through the drill at the same time. When the defensive ends are running through the drill, the coach should employ a fullback. The end and the tackle can work together on both the strong and the weak side, or they can work in their own groups.

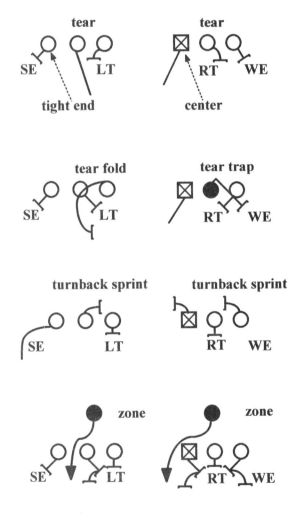

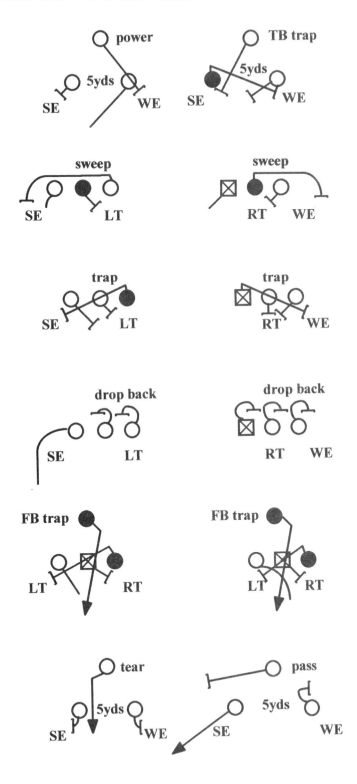

LINEBACKER READ DRILLS

These two drills need to be run every day during two-a-day practices and in the early part of the season. The coach should not add the offensive line until the players are comfortable with the first drill. These drills do not employ a quarterback or a ball. The linebackers should be able to locate the ball by reacting to their keys.

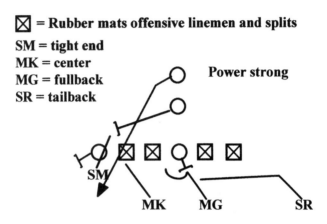

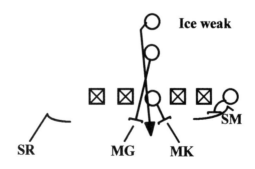

LINEBACKER READ DRILLS (CONT.)

SM = tight end
MK = center
MG = fullback
SR = tailback

Sprint pass weak

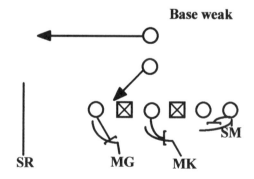

Base weak

SR   MG   MK   SM

DEFENSIVE FRONT AND LINEBACKER READ DRILLS

For this drill, a team that has both a defensive front coach and a linebacker coach can split up the players into two groups. The tackles and the inside linebackers can work on inside run reads. The outside linebackers and the ends can work on option and run reads. Another possibility is for the outside linebacker to join the secondary to work on two-deep coverage, while the defensive front and the inside linebackers work on run reads. The coach also has the option of having the front and the linebacker working together on run reads. The only drill in which a quarterback or a ball is utilized is the drill that works on option reads.

INSIDE LINEBACKER & TACKLES

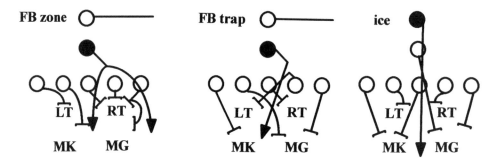

OUTSIDE LINEBACKER & ENDS

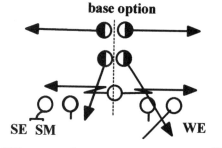

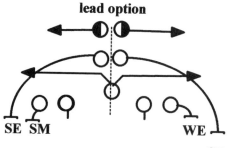

When running this drill run one side, then the other.

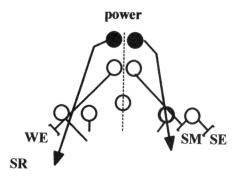

INSIDE LINEBACKER & FRONT

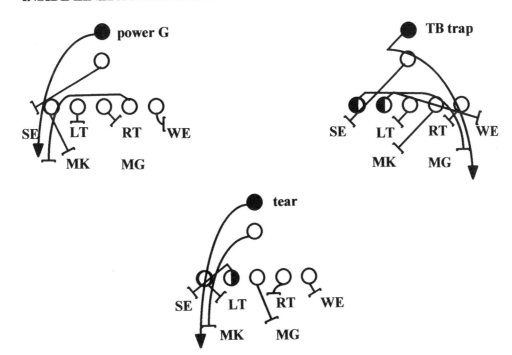

FRONT & LINEBACKER

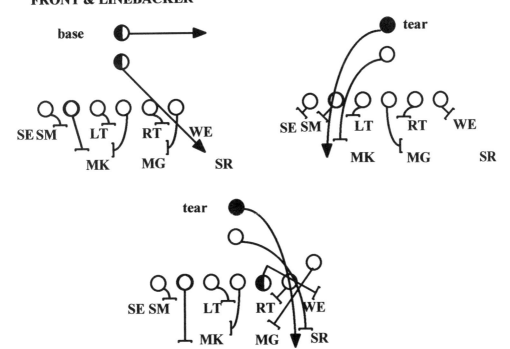

SECONDARY RUN/PASS READ DRILLS

The players in the secondary should read through the linemen for a run/pass read as they take their read steps. As the play develops, the secondary should pick up the quarterback, the backfield action, and the receivers and then react to the play. This drill should be run every day during two-a-day practices and also early in the season.

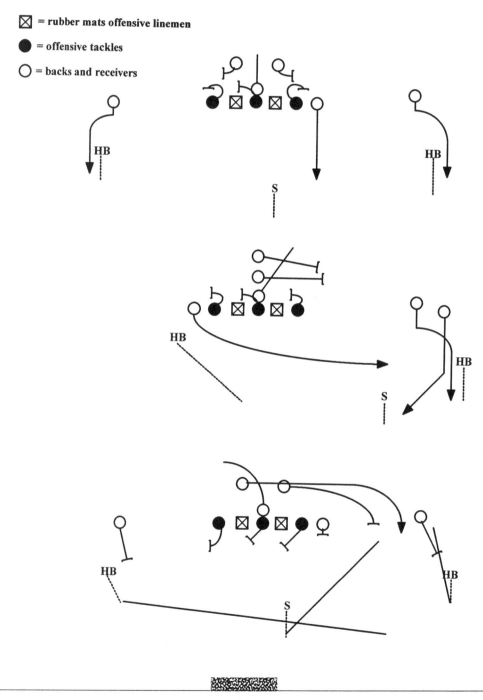

= rubber mats offensive linemen

= offensive tackles

= backs and receivers

SECONDARY AND OUTSIDE LINEBACKERS RUN/PASS READ DRILLS

This drill is especially helpful to a coach who is working on his team's two-deep coverage and reads. The drill works on alignment, spacing, funnel technique, and run/pass reads. The drill can also be run using the inside linebackers.

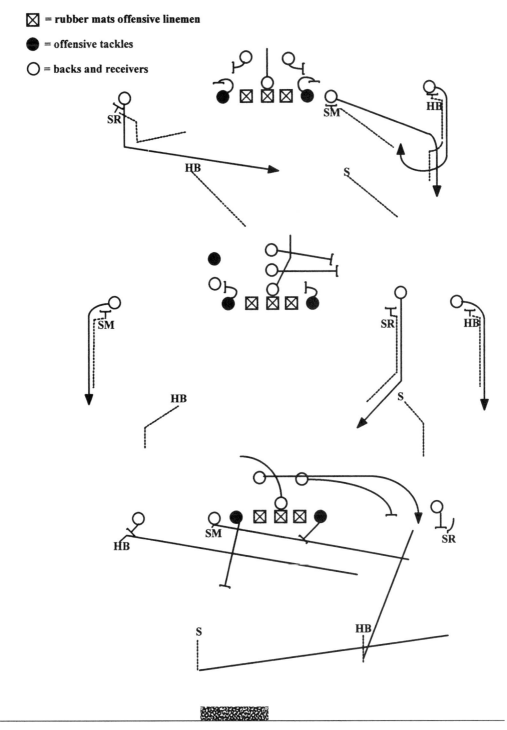

CHAPTER 7

Playbook

Do the Little Things Right, and the Big Things Will Take Care of Themselves

TEAM GOALS

- Make the playoffs
- Win the conference championship
- Play in a bowl game
- Win the Region IV championship
- Win the national championship

DEFENSIVE TEAM GOALS

- Our defense must not allow any opponent to complete a long pass for an "easy" touchdown.
- Our defense must not allow any opponent to make a run of over 20 yards.
- Our defense must not allow the opponent to score by way of the run from within our 10-yard line.
- Our defense must hold the opponent to under 240 yards of total offense.
- Our defense must hold our opponent to under 60 offensive plays (punts not included).
- Our defense must intercept at least 1 pass for every 10 thrown.
- Our defense must average 10 yards on returns of interceptions and punts.
- Our defense must hold our opponent to less than 15 yards per kickoff return.
- Our defense must either score or turn the ball over to our offense inside the opponent's 25-yard line.
- Our defense must force the opponent to fumble three times.
- Our defense must produce six plays of negative yardage.
- Our defense must hold our opponent to 10 points or less.

DEFENSIVE POSITIONS

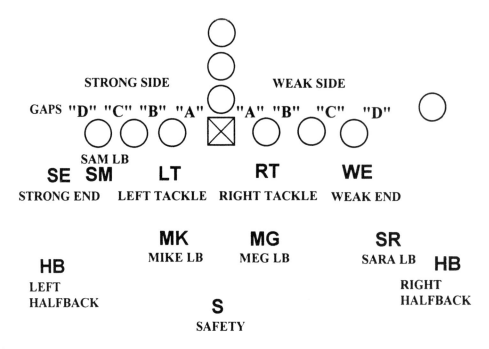

STRENGTH AND COLOR CALL

Strength Call: We will make the strength call to the offensive tight end. If there are either two tight ends or no tight end, the strength will depend on our scouting report and our game plan.

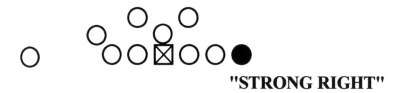

"STRONG RIGHT"

Color Call: We will make a color call after the strength call is made. The color call will be made to the two-receiver side.

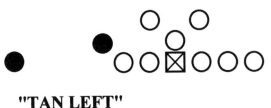

"TAN LEFT"

DEFENSIVE HUDDLE

BALL

MK

SE LT SM RT WE
HB S SR MG HB

1. The Sam linebacker will form the huddle two yards off the ball.

2. The players in the front row will keep their heads up and their hands on their knees; the players in the back row will stand up straight, with their hands behind their back.

3. The Mike linebacker will make the defensive call and give the break.

BALL

MK

LT SM RT
SE SR WE
MG

HB S HB

After the break:

1. The tackles will go to one knee on their side of the ball.

2. The secondary will go to its normal area of the field.

3. The defensive ends will move in behind the tackles.

4. Everyone should be looking at the offensive huddle.

5. When the tight end and the other receivers break from the offensive huddle, Sam and Mike will give the strength call.

6. Everyone sprints to his alignment as the Sara linebacker and the secondary give their color call.

COMMUNICATION

When we speak of communication, we are not referring to the trash talk or the verbal contests some players get themselves into. When a player gets caught up in a verbal battle with an opponent, three things happen—and all of them are bad: (1) The player's focus changes from doing what it takes to get the ball back to the offense, to getting even with someone. (2) The time spent by the player communicating with his opponent detracts from the time he should be spending communicating with his teammates. (3) Any verbal contest becomes conspicuous to the officials, and any close call is going to go against the player. The end result is that the player is coming out of the game. PERFORM, DON'T INFORM, and people will get the point much quicker.

Players must communicate with one another at all times during the game, both on and off the field. They must be able to understand each other. It is very important that coaches and players use and understand the same language. When a player hears "blue right" or "tear," a mental picture of an offensive formation and a blocking scheme should appear. Before and during the offensive play, the whole team must communicate. Our ability to win over a superior opponent will depend on our ability to communicate with one another. On every down, whether in a game or in a practice, there are current "calls" that must be made which inform the players of their responsibilities and assignments.

Following is a list of calls and information that must be exchanged before and during a play:

- STRENGTH CALL: The SAM and MIKE linebackers make the strength call to the tight end—"strong left, strong left."

- COLOR CALL: The SECONDARY and the SARA linebacker make the color call to the two-receiver side—"blue left, blue left."

- BACKFIELD SET CALL: If necessary, the MIKE and MEG linebackers and the SAFETY will make the backfield set call—"ace, ace."

- MOTION CALL: The SARA linebacker and the SECONDARY make a motion call when either receivers or backs go in motion—"motion, motion."

- COVERAGE CALL: If we need to change our coverage to the current offensive formation, the SAFETY will make the call—"ace, ace, check III, check III."

- RED CALL: Those times when we need to get out of running a stunt, the LINEBACKERS will make the call—"red, red."

- RUN/PASS CALL: When a defensive player reads the play, he will let everyone know by making either a run or a pass call—"pass, pass."

- BALL CALL: If a player sees that the ball is either on the ground or in the air, he will make a ball call—"ball, ball."

- PLAY CALL: Anyone who reads the play will yell out the type of play—"reverse, reverse."

- CROSS CALL: When LINEBACKERS see receivers running crossing routes under our coverage, they will give a cross call—"cross, cross."

- ROUTE CALL: The SECONDARY calls out the receiver's routes to the under coverage—"post, post."

- BINGO CALL: Anytime we intercept a pass, we give a "bingo" call to the closest sideline so we can set up a return—"bingo left, bingo left."

- OPTION RESPONSIBILITY: On every down, those involved in covering the option must tell each other their option responsibility. Example: The SAM linebacker tells the STRONG END, "I've got #2," and the end tells the SAM linebacker, "I've got #3." Those players who have an option responsibility should let the players around them know what it is!

KEYS

Our defense has been successful in stopping any and all offenses. The reason for our success has been our ability to determine what the offensive play is going to be—before or just after the offense has taken its first step. We are able to accomplish quick recognition of offensive plays by using a series of keys. We use five different keys to determine where the ball is going before and during the play. On most offensive plays, we will only need one or two keys in order to know what the play is.

FORMATION AND ALIGNMENT: Offenses can be very predictable with their formation and alignment. We will form a game plan around these offensive tendencies. Two examples of a team's tendencies would be their habit of passing exclusively out of split backs and their habit of running the ball out of the "I." The individual positions in an offensive formation can tip the play. A few examples include a split receiver taking a wider split than normal when he is going to run the "post" pattern, an offensive lineman sitting flat in his stance when he is going to pass block or pull, and a running back who is always aligned deeper whenever he is going to get the ball. I have yet to see a team that didn't tip something.

PRE-SNAP KEYS: Each position is given one of three pre-snap keys: (1) the foot of the "near back," (2) the helmet of the offensive player whom the defensive player is aligned on, and (3) an uncovered lineman. We will key the ball for movement. At the snap of the ball, this key will get us moving in the right direction to make the play or defeat any immediate block.

BACKFIELD ACTION: We will read this key while we are on the move to the ball. Backfield action will determine the direction and type of play and give us a run/pass read.

BLOCKING SCHEMES: Run or pass, there are only a few different ways the offense can block a play. Therefore, blocking schemes can be a good key in determining the offensive play. There will be times when a defensive player will able to determine the play before he picks up the backfield action just by seeing how he is being blocked and by whom. The defense must learn and understand the offensive blocking schemes; if he cannot do this, a player is going to have a hard time playing our defense.

BALL LEVEL: The depth of the ball during the play will indicate what type of play the offense is running.

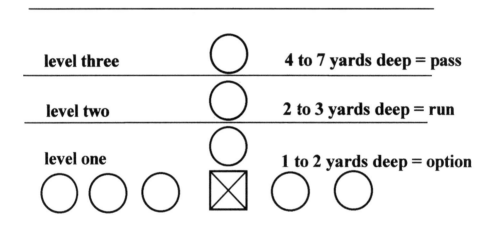

level three	◯	**4 to 7 yards deep = pass**
level two	◯	**2 to 3 yards deep = run**
level one	◯	**1 to 2 yards deep = option**

The keys should be used to find the ball and get the defensive player moving to it. Players should think of the keys in two groups: FORMATION & ALIGNMENT, and PRE-SNAP. These keys will provide a good idea of where the play is going and also get the defense moving in the right direction. BACKFIELD ACTION, BLOCKING SCHEMES, and BALL LEVEL will take the defense to the ball. Our players cannot stand around looking for the ball—they must read on the run!

BACKFIELD SETS, RECEIVER SETS, COLOR, AND ALIGNMENT

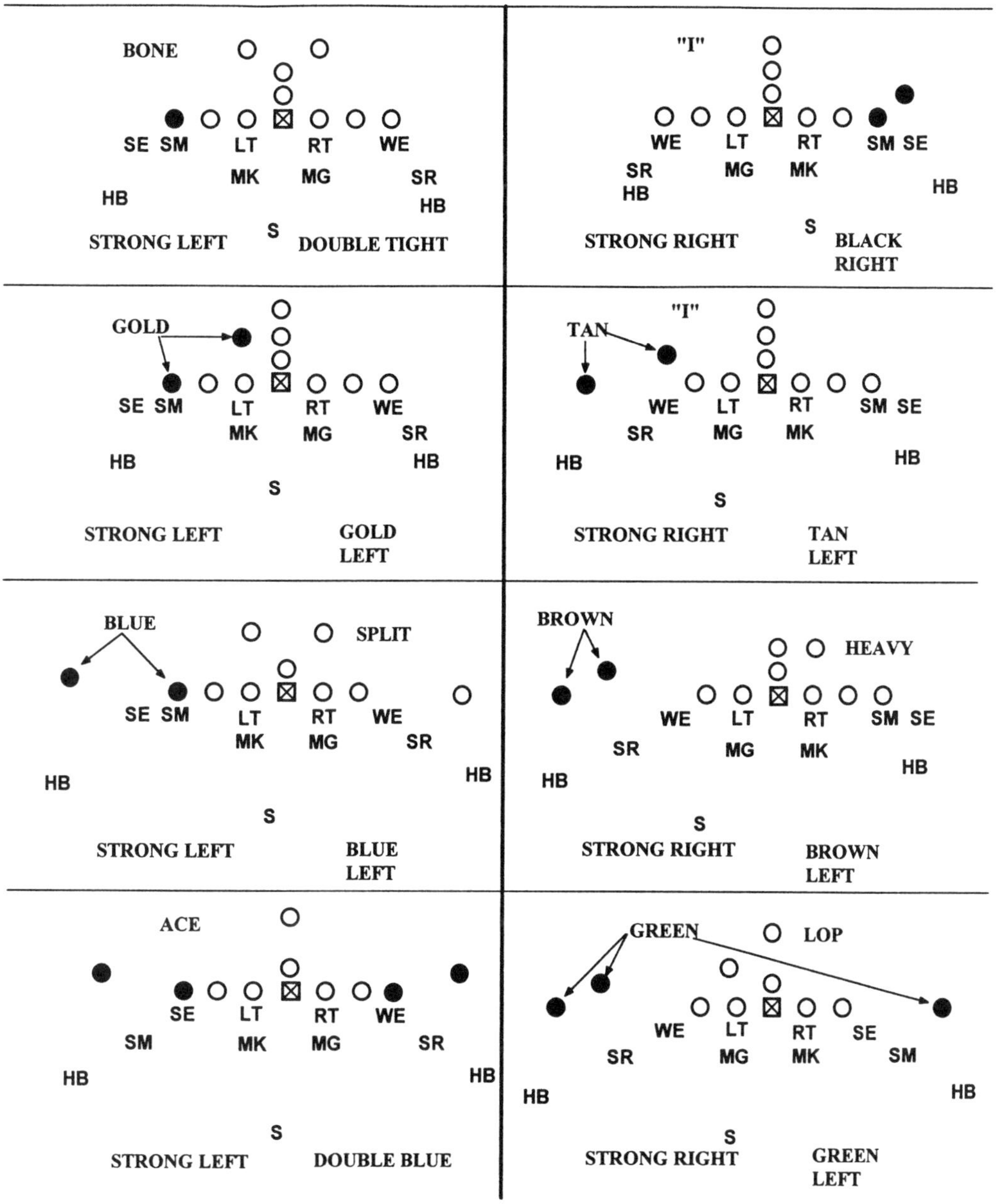

BONE

SE SM LT RT WE
MK MG SR
HB   HB
S
STRONG LEFT   DOUBLE TIGHT

"I"

WE LT RT SM SE
SR MG MK
HB   HB
S
STRONG RIGHT   BLACK RIGHT

GOLD

SE SM LT RT WE
MK MG SR
HB   HB
S
STRONG LEFT   GOLD LEFT

TAN   **"I"**

WE LT RT SM SE
SR MG MK
HB   HB
S
STRONG RIGHT   TAN LEFT

BLUE   SPLIT

SE SM LT RT WE
MK MG SR
HB   HB
S
STRONG LEFT   BLUE LEFT

BROWN   HEAVY

WE LT RT SM SE
SR MG MK
HB   HB
S
STRONG RIGHT   BROWN LEFT

ACE

SE LT RT WE
SM MK MG SR
HB   HB
S
STRONG LEFT   DOUBLE BLUE

GREEN   LOP

WE LT RT SE SM
SR MG MK
HB   HB
S
STRONG RIGHT   GREEN LEFT

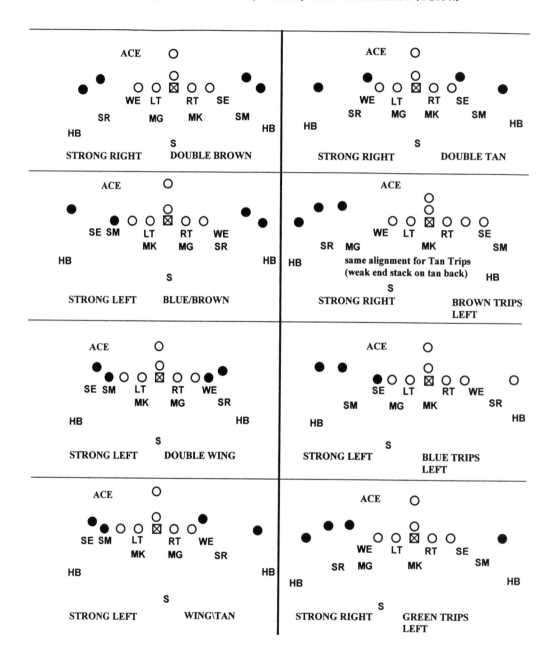

RUN SUPPORT

Defensive football is very simple and quite unlike offensive football. With the defense, everybody is after the same person—and that is the guy with the ball! Defensive players must do just a few things when stopping an offensive run play: (1) Find the ball quickly while on the move. In fact, a player is better off moving in the wrong direction than not moving at all! (2) Always close quickly to the ball, while under control. Player should never stop moving their feet, slow down, or wait for the ball to come to them. (3) Always take a force angle to the ball. The defense should overplay the angle from the inside or the outside. The defensive players should take away the ball carrier's options and force him to either redirect or come over the top of the defender. It is important for the defense to trap the ball. (4) When playing off blocks and moving to the ball, players should keep their shoulders square to the line of scrimmage.

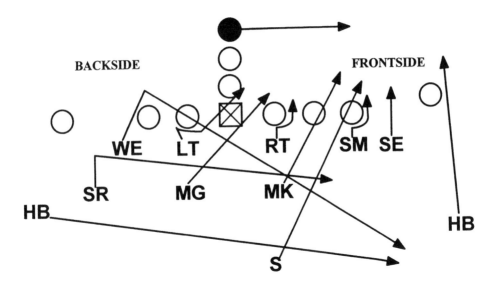

FRONT SIDE

Halfback: Forces the play from outside in; looks for the play to bounce outside.

Strong end: Forces the play inside; closes from outside in.

Sam linebacker: Closes "C" gap; forces the play from the inside out.

Right tackle: Closes "B" gap; forces the play from the inside out.

Mike linebacker: Closes from the inside out, working from "A" to "B" to "C" gaps.

Safety: Works upfield through the "Alley"; closes from inside out.

BACK SIDE

Left tackle: Squeezes "B" gap down through "A"; plays across the face of the blocker and closes the play down from the back side.

Meg linebacker: Plays through the head of the offensive center; closes from "A" gap, working to the outside; looks for cutback and does not over-pursue.

Weak end: Crosses the line of scrimmage; checks for reverse, bootleg, or broken play. Takes a cutoff angle to stop the play if it breaks.

Sara linebacker: Checks for reverse, bootleg, or broken play. Takes a cutoff angle to the ball if the play breaks.

Halfback: Takes a cutoff angle to the ball to stop the play if it breaks.

READS: PASS BLOCKING AND READING THE PASS PLAY

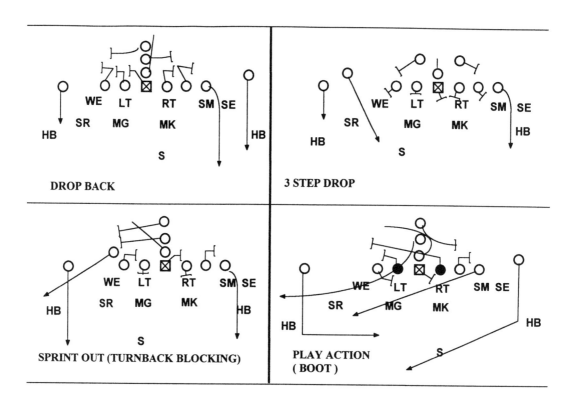

DROP BACK

3 STEP DROP

SPRINT OUT (TURNBACK BLOCKING)

PLAY ACTION
(BOOT)

Before and during a pass play, the offense will tip off how they are attacking the defense. Linemen, receivers, backs, and the quarterback all have tendencies that are not difficult to spot, if you know what to look for.

Linemen: When aligned to pass block, they will sit flat in their stance, pop up, and give ground at the snap.

Receivers: The number of receivers in the game is a tip-off; when they are thinking pass, teams will substitute wide receivers for running backs. Receivers will take their splits, depending on the type of pass pattern they are running. (Example: If the receiver is running an "out" route, he will align closer to the ball than normal. Likewise, if the receiver is running a "post" route, he will widen his split.) Most pass routes have only one cut. When making a cut, the receiver will shorten his stride and drop his hips. An important point to keep in mind about pass patterns is that, on average, the ball is on the receiver's hands by the time the receiver has taken his sixth step after making his pattern cut.

Backs: Running backs will sit flat in their stance when they are going to pass block and align closer to the line of scrimmage when they are going to run a pass route.

Quarterback: How the quarterback carries the ball will tell the defense the direction, distance, and when he is going to release the ball. The front shoulder of the quarterback will point in the direction that he is throwing the ball. If his front shoulder is higher than his back shoulder, the ball is going deep. If his shoulders are level, then he is throwing in the short or medium range. When the quarterback is ready to throw the ball, he will take his front hand off the ball to start his throwing motion.

BLOCKING SCHEMES

The offense can block our defense only so many ways. We must be able to recognize an offensive play by the blocking scheme. Also, we must be able to communicate to one another by using terms that will give us a visual image of how a play is being blocked. These diagrams illustrate the most common blocking schemes that teams will use to block us.

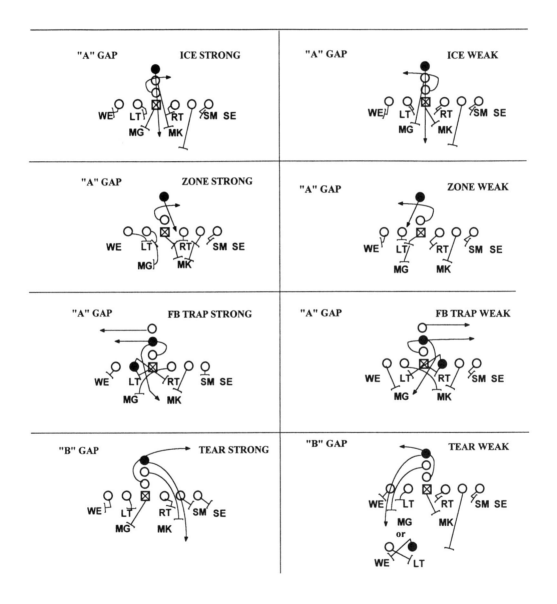

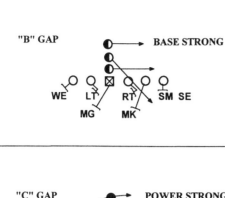

"B" GAP — BASE STRONG

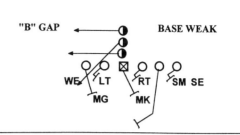

"B" GAP — BASE WEAK

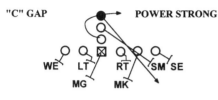

"C" GAP — POWER STRONG

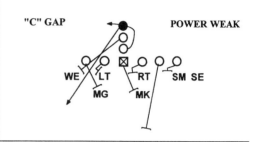

"C" GAP — POWER WEAK

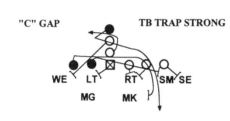

"C" GAP — TB TRAP STRONG

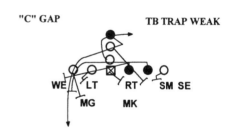

"C" GAP — TB TRAP WEAK

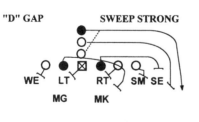

"D" GAP — SWEEP STRONG

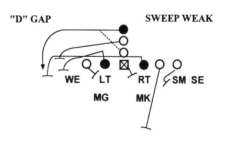

"D" GAP — SWEEP WEAK

CHAPTER 8

Base Defense, FIST III

FIST III LEFT AND RIGHT TACKLES

BLUE RIGHT ○   ○
         ○
○   ○ ○ ⊠ ○ ○ ○   ○
        LT   RT
 	
              STRONG RIGHT
	TAN RIGHT ○ ○
	         ○ ○
	○ ○ ○ ⊠ ○ ○ ○ ○
	        LT RT
	
	              STRONG LEFT

BROWN LEFT ○   ○
        ○
○ ○   ○ ○ ⊠ ○ ○ ○
        LT   RT
 	
              STRONG RIGHT
	GREEN RIGHT ○ ○
	          ○
	○ ○ ○ ⊠ ○ ○ ○ ○
	        LT RT
	
	              STRONG LEFT

STANCE: Both tackles should use a three-point stance, with their outside foot slightly back (heel to toe). Their weight should be forward on their fingertips, and their back should be flat. Their feet should be shoulder-width apart, with their heels up and their weight on the balls of their feet.

ALIGNMENT: The tackles should head-up the offensive guard, crowding the ball. (We may adjust their alignment to nose on the outside shoulder of the offensive guard.)

KEY: The tackles' key is the helmet of the offensive guard, as well as the blocking schemes to the backfield action. They should use the ball for movement.

RESPONSIBILITY: The tackles should play the run first and the pass second. If the play is a run, they are responsible for "B" gap and should squeeze the play down from "B" gap to "A" gap. If the play is an "option," they will have #1 (the dive back). If the play is a pass, they are responsible for the inside pass rush and draw. As defensive tackles, they will see two types of blocks, both of which they must play and defeat on every down: the "drive," or "reach," block and the "trap" block. It is very important to our defense that the tackles are able to control the offensive guard and defeat those blocks.

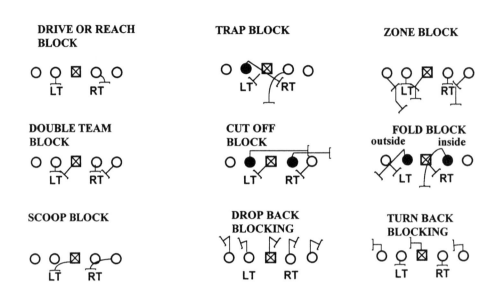

DRIVE OR REACH BLOCK

TRAP BLOCK

ZONE BLOCK

DOUBLE TEAM BLOCK

CUT OFF BLOCK

FOLD BLOCK
outside   inside

SCOOP BLOCK

DROP BACK BLOCKING

TURN BACK BLOCKING

FIST III STRONG AND WEAK ENDS

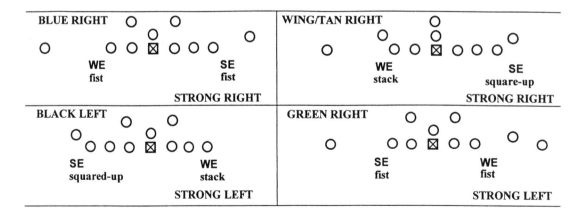

BLUE RIGHT	WING/TAN RIGHT
WE fist SE fist	WE stack SE square-up
STRONG RIGHT	STRONG RIGHT
BLACK LEFT	GREEN RIGHT
SE squared-up WE stack	SE fist WE fist
STRONG LEFT	STRONG LEFT

STANCE: The defensive ends must be able to play out of two stances—a two-point stance and a three-point stance. When using the two-point stance, their inside foot should be back, with most of their weight on their front foot. Their feet should be inside their shoulders about 6 to 10 inches apart. Their front foot is the drive foot, and their back foot is the balance foot. Their stance is not a contact type of stance; thus their upper body should be relaxed and poised for movement. The three-point stance, which we will call "STACK," is a stance that we want the tackles to use for making contact. In the three-point stance, their inside foot should be slightly back (heel to toe), with their weight on their fingertips and front foot. Their back should be flat. On a few occasions, we will call on them to use a "SQUARED-UP" stance. The only time we will use this stance is to a "WING SET," and, even then, only on the strong side (see the "WING/TAN" set). The "squared-up" stance is a two-point stance in which the player's feet and shoulders are parallel to the line of scrimmage.

ALIGNMENT: The strong and weak ends must be able to use four types of alignment: FIST, STACK, SQUARED-UP, and "40." We will use these alignments to adjust to the different offensive formations from our FIST III defense. We will also use these four alignments to align in a different defensive formation. Both ends need to know only these four alignments and how to use them. Their alignment will depend on the defense called and the offensive formation.

FIST: In this two-point stance, the ends should have their inside foot a yard outside of the offensive tight end or tackle, on a line that is at a 45-degree angle to the line of scrimmage. They should be running through the stance of the offensive back to their side and crowding the ball.

STACK: In this three-point stance, the ends should be head-up the tight end or tan back and be crowding the ball. When FIST is the defensive call, we use the "STACK" alignment only to the weak side—when the offensive formation has either a tight end or a tan back.

SQUARED-UP: The ends should assume this two-point parallel stance, head-up the wingback, and be crowding the ball. The only time we will use this alignment is when we see a wingback on the strong side.

"40": The ends should assume this three-point stance on the outside shoulder of the offensive tackle. Their inside foot should be aligned on the outside foot of the offensive tackle, and they should crowd the ball. The "40" alignment will be used in two of our other defenses, but we will use this alignment as an adjustment for the defensive ends against some offensive formations. Our scouting report and game plan will dictate our use of this alignment.

FIST ALIGNMENT

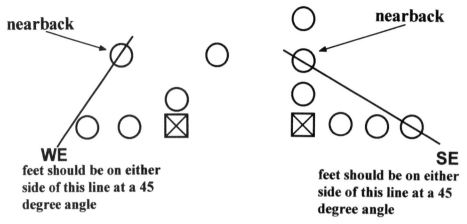

nearback

WE
feet should be on either
side of this line at a 45
degree angle

nearback

SE
feet should be on either
side of this line at a 45
degree angle

KEY: The ends will key the ball for movement, no matter what the offensive alignment is. The defensive ends will use one of two keys, depending on their alignment: the outside foot of the "near back" (the offensive running back closest to a player's side) and the helmet of the offensive player they are aligned on.

FOOT OF THE NEAR BACK: When in the "FIST" alignment, the ends will key through the down linemen, to the foot of the near back. They will use this key to get them moving to the ball. The ends' steps will depend on the direction of the near back's first step. After the first step of the near back, the ends should pick up the backfield action, the blocking scheme, and the level of the ball.

HELMET OF OFFENSIVE PLAYER: When using any of the other three alignments (stack, squared-up, or "40"), the ends should key the helmet to pick up the blocking scheme, the backfield action, and the level of the ball.

RESPONSIBILITIES: The responsibilities of the defensive ends are simple; they will depend on alignment and which position they are playing—strong end or weak end.

STRONG END: Run responsibility for the strong end will be "D" gap. He should close everything down from the outside in. If the play is to his opposite side, he should first make sure it isn't a bootleg, a reverse, or a broken play, and then take a cutoff pursuit angle. If the offensive play is "option," he will have #3 (the pitch). If pass shows, he has outside pass rush and contain on the quarterback. HE MUST KEEP CONTAIN! The only exception would be if he was in a "switch" position. A "SWITCH POSITION" will occur only when the offensive formation has no tight end. The SAM linebacker will make a "switch" call, which will change the strong end's gap responsibility to "C" gap and #2 (the quarterback) on option plays; everything else is played the same.

WEAK END: Run responsibility for the weak end is "C" gap. He should close everything down from the outside in. If the play is to his opposite side, he should first make sure the play isn't a bootleg, a reverse, or a broken play, and then take a cutoff pursuit angle. If the weak end is in a "stack" alignment, he cannot let the tight end or the tan back block him. He should play the block straight up and not pick a side, and he should then work to "C" gap. His option responsibility is #2 (the quarterback). If pass shows, he can have outside pass rush and contain on the quarterback. THE WEAK END MUST KEEP CONTAIN!

COMMON BLOCKING SCHEMES AGAINST THE ENDS

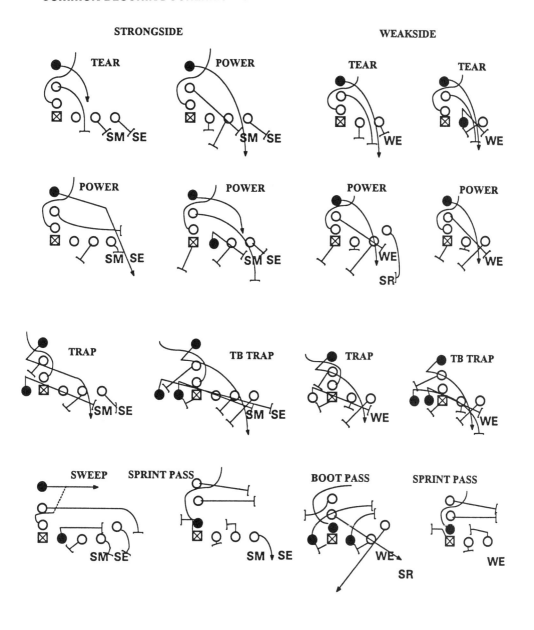

FIST III SAM AND SARA LINEBACKERS

```
TAN LEFT          O      O              BROWN RIGHT          O      O
              O      O                                          O             O
  O      O   O  ⊠ O O O                   O  O  O  ⊠ O  O              O
         WE            SM  SE             SE  SM           WE
     SR                                                        SR
                     STRONG RIGHT                           STRONG LEFT
```

```
BLUE TRIPS        O                     GREEN TRIPS RIGHT    O
  RIGHT           O                                          O             O      O
  O      O  O  ⊠ O O O      O  O            O      O  O  ⊠ O  O
         WE          SE  switch                 switch   SE         WE
     SR                   SM                        SM                    SR
                     STRONG RIGHT                           STRONG LEFT
```

STANCE:

    SAM LINEBACKER: His feet should be shoulder-width apart, with his heels clearing the ground and parallel to the line of scrimmage. His weight should be on his outside foot. His hips should be bent halfway between a sitting and a standing position. His hands should be carried just outside of his knees in a relaxed and comfortable position, ready to deliver a blow into the tight end.

    SARA LINEBACKER: His feet should be shoulder-width apart, with his heels clearing the ground and parallel to the line of scrimmage. His weight should be evenly distributed on his feet. His hips should be bent halfway between a sitting and a standing position. His hands should be carried just outside of his knees in a relaxed and comfortable position.

ALIGNMENT:

    SAM LINEBACKER: When the offensive formation has a tight end, the Sam linebacker will align head-up the tight end on the strong side, crowding the ball. His alignment will change only when we need to adjust to the offensive formation. Our adjustment will be one of three alignments, depending on the offensive formation: (1) When there is no tight end in the offensive formation, Sam should align on the one-receiver side, halfway between the offensive split end and the tackle (GREEN, GREEN TRIPS). (2) The inside shoulder of the inside wide receiver to Sam's side (DOUBLE BROWN, BLUE TRIPS). (3) Stacked a yard outside of the strong end (DOUBLE TAN). The depth of these alignments will be four yards.

    SARA LINEBACKER: His alignment will be to the weak side in one of four different alignments at a depth of four yards. If the offensive formation has two tight ends or tan backs (BLACK, TAN, DOUBLE TAN), Sara should stack a yard outside of the weak end at a depth of four yards. If there is just one wide receiver to his side (PINK, BLUE, DOUBLE BLUE), Sara should align halfway between the offensive tackle or the tight end and the wide receiver. If there are two wide receivers to his side (BROWN, DOUBLE BROWN), he should align on the inside shoulder of the inside receiver four yards deep. If there are three wide receivers to his side (GREEN TRIPS), he should align on the inside shoulder of the middle receiver. Our game plan and scouting report may change the alignment of the Sara linebacker.

KEY:

SAM LINEBACKER: When aligned over the tight end, he should key his helmet and the ball for movement. Sam should key his helmet in order to see if the tight end is blocking him. Once he has made sure the tight end is not a blocking threat, he should pick up the backfield action, the blocking scheme, and the level of the ball. When Sam's alignment is four yards deep, he should key the outside foot of the near back. The first step of the near back will get Sam moving in the direction of the ball. He should then pick up the backfield action, the blocking scheme, and the level of the ball.

SARA LINEBACKER: Sara should key the outside foot of the near back to his side. The first step of the near back will get Sara moving in the direction of the ball. Next, he should pick up the backfield action, the blocking scheme, and the level of the ball.

RESPONSIBILITIES:

SAM LINEBACKER: He calls the defensive huddle and makes the strength call to the tight end. If the offensive formation has no tight end, Sam should make the strength call to the one-receiver side (GREEN, GREEN TRIPS). If the offensive formation is balanced (DOUBLE TAN, DOUBLE BROWN, DOUBLE BLUE), he should make the strength call to the short side of the field or to the right. (Our game plan and our scouting report may change Sam's alignment, as well as the strength.) When Sam's alignment is on the tight end and the offense shows run, he has "C" gap, and he should assume the tight end is blocking him on every down. Sam should play the tight end straight up, he should not pick a side, and he should close down "C" gap and be in position to help if the play bounces outside. If the play is to Sam's opposite side, he should take a pursuit angle looking for a cutback. If the play is an option, he has #2 (the quarterback). His pass responsibility is the flat. When the alignment is four yards deep (no tight end), he must first make a "switch" call. This call will inform the strong end that Sam is switching run and option responsibilities with him. As a result, Sam will have "D" gap and #3 on the option (the pitch). He should play run from outside in; his pass responsibility is the flat.

SARA LINEBACKER: He will make the color call after the strength call is made. On running plays, Sara is responsible for "D" gap, and he should close it down from the outside in. He should not pursue inside until he is sure the play isn't bouncing outside. If the play is to the opposite side, he should take a cutoff pursuit angle and look for a cutback. If option shows, he has #3 (the pitch). His pass responsibility is the flat.

COMMON BLOCKING SCHEMES AGAINST OUTSIDE LINEBACKERS

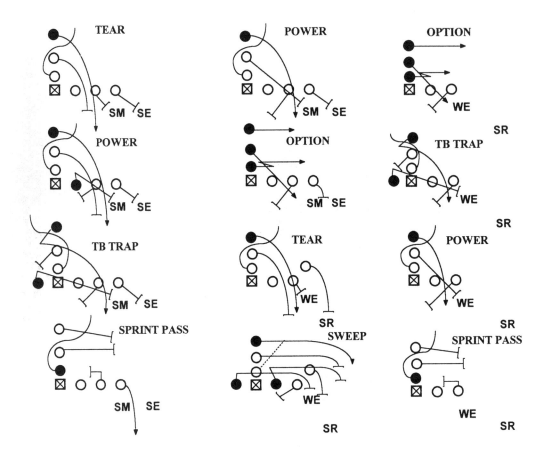

FIST III MIKE AND MEG LINEBACKERS

BLUE RIGHT	BLUE TRIPS
MG MK	MG MK
STRONG RIGHT	STRONG LEFT
BROWN LEFT	GREEN TRIPS
MG MK	MK MG
STRONG RIGHT	STRONG LEFT

STANCE: Both the Mike and Meg linebackers should assume a two-point stance, with their feet parallel and shoulder-width apart. Their weight should be evenly distributed, with their heels clearing the ground. They should be bent at the hips halfway between a sitting and a standing position. Their hands and arms should be carried in front of them in a relaxed and comfortable position.

ALIGNMENT: The MIKE linebacker will align to the strong side of the offensive formation, while the MEG linebacker will align to the weak side. Their inside foot should split the stance of the offensive guard at a depth of four to four and a half yards deep.

KEYS: They should key the outside foot of the near back. If the foot of the near back is not visible because of his alignment, they should key his helmet. Whenever possible, they should key his foot, because by doing so, they will get a better jump on the play. They should key the ball for movement.

RESPONSIBILITIES: The Mike linebacker will make the strength call and any other calls he is responsible for (see "Communication" section of the playbook). The inside linebackers are responsible for "A" gap, as well as all running plays from the inside to the outside. Mike should read the first step of the near back; when the near back steps toward him, Mike should mirror his step and attack the line of scrimmage, working from "A" gap to "B," "C," and "D" gaps. Instead of working under blocks, he should work through the outside half of the blocker while on the move, moving from the inside out. If the near back steps away from him, Mike should work through the "A" gaps and take the center's block (or any other block) straight up without picking a side. He should pursue the play from the back side, but he should not over-pursue. He should look for the cutback. If the play is an option, Mike has #1 (the dive). His pass responsibility is the curl to the seam, the hook, and the hole.

COMMON BLOCKING SCHEMES AGAINST INSIDE LINEBACKERS

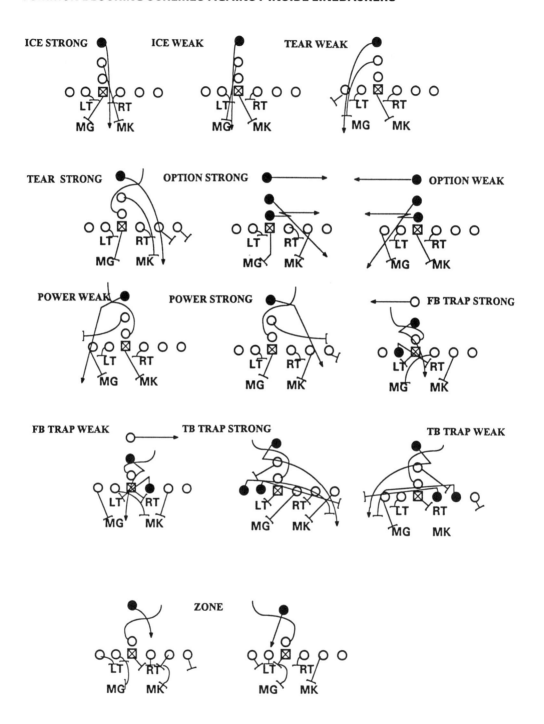

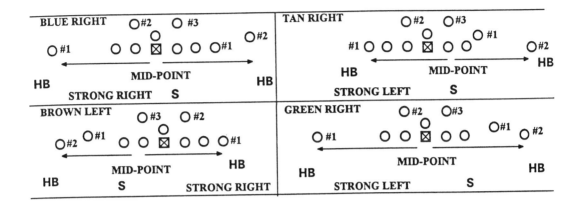

STANCE: The secondary players should assume a two-point stance, with their inside foot kept back (for the safety, the foot to the wide side of the field should be kept back). Their weight should be on their front foot, and their knees should be bent and squeezed together. Their hips should be high, and their chin should be out over their toes. Their feet should be heel-to-toe about six inches apart.

ALIGNMENT:

HALFBACKS: The halfbacks will align on the widest receiver to their side of the offensive formation. When aligning on a wide receiver, their alignment should be seven yards deep and two yards outside of the receiver. If the formation is closed (this means that the widest receiver is a tight end), their alignment will be five yards deep and two yards outside of the tight end. Because they will see so many different types of formations in different areas of the field, the halfbacks will follow a few simple rules that will change their alignment slightly. These rules will put them in the best position to make the play.

- Numbers Rule: Anytime they have a single receiver that aligns on or outside of the "numbers," the halfbacks will change their alignment to the inside, seven yards deep and one yard to the inside.

- Bracket Rule: Anytime the offense has two or more split receivers to the same side, we want to "bracket" the receivers from the inside (safety's alignment) to the outside with the alignment of our halfbacks. Our under coverage will also help in bracketing the receivers. The idea is to cut down on the space that the receivers will have available to run routes by our alignment. The halfbacks will align seven yards deep and one yard outside of the widest receiver. We will use this alignment even if the receiver is on or outside of the numbers.

SAFETY: The safety's alignment will depend on the offensive formation. A simple rule of thumb that will put the safety in the best position to make the play is to be 12 yards deep on the "midpoint" between the widest receiver to each side. The safety should think of himself and the widest receivers forming a 12-yard-high pyramid with the safety at the top of the pyramid. Most of the time, this rule will help the safety put himself in the proper position; however, there are exceptions. When two or more split receivers are put to one side, the safety may have to cheat beyond the midpoint if the receivers stretch the field. How far the safety must cheat his alignment will depend on the position of the ball (middle or hash) on the field and the wide receivers' alignment. The safety needs to remember to cut down the space the receivers have available for running routes past the safety's alignment. An example of when to cheat alignment and when not to is as follows: When two receivers split into the sideline, the safety should stay on the field's midpoint; the sideline will cut down the space. When two receivers split to the open side of the field, the safety should cheat his alignment to the receivers. The halfback, the Sara linebacker, and the safety should "bracket" the receivers. They should cheat their alignment until they are in position to make the play on the inside route if all go deep.

KEYS: The secondary's order of keys will be (1) the nearest uncovered offensive lineman, (2) the backfield action, (3) the level of the ball, (4) the quarterback, and (5) the receivers. As the ball is snapped and the play develops, players must backpedal until they determine if the play is run or pass. They should play the pass first and the run second. If linemen are releasing downfield for a block, the backfield action and the level of the ball will give the secondary a "run" read. If linemen are pass blocking, or if backs are blocking or releasing, the quarterback and receivers will give the secondary a pass read. When a pass play is recognized, the secondary should key the receivers and the quarterback's release of the ball. They should read through the #1 receiver to the quarterback. Picking up the #1 receiver's route can tell the secondary a lot about the other receivers' routes. The secondary players should not look at just one receiver's route or at the quarterback. They must keep everything in view and see the field so they will have time to react.

RECEIVER NUMBERING:

#1 RECEIVER: The first receiver to each side, on or off the line of scrimmage, closest to the ball.

#2 RECEIVER: The next receiver to the outside of the #1 receiver on each side, or the nearest back in the backfield.

#3 RECEIVER: The next receiver to the outside of the #2 receiver, or the nearest back in the backfield.

#4 RECEIVER: The nearest back in the backfield.

RESPONSIBILITIES: The secondary's main job is to defend against the deep pass and stop any running play that breaks. The secondary should keep in mind that a missed tackle on any run or pass will mean a touchdown.

PASS: Three deep zones split the field into thirds. The halfbacks are responsible for the outside thirds and the safety for the middle third. The halfbacks and the safety should play over the top of the deepest route in their zone and break up on routes in the under zones. They should stay in their backpedal until the receiver breaks their "cushion" (they should keep deeper than the receiver by three to four yards while in their backpedal); they should "zone flip" (drop their hips and turn upfield toward the quarterback), running over the top of the receiver and pinning him to the nearest sideline. (RED ZONE RULE: The "red zone" is the area inside our 20-yard line. When the offense has the ball in our red zone, the secondary should play under the deepest route in our zone in man coverage. We will employ this type of coverage only when the ball is in this zone.)

RUN:
   HALFBACKS: When run shows, STAY OUTSIDE; close the play down from the outside in. If the run is away from the halfbacks, they should take a pursuit angle to cut the play off in case it breaks.

   SAFETY: When run shows, the safety should work upfield through the "alley" (the area on the field which opens up outside of the offensive guard/tackle area), closing from the inside out.

CHAPTER 9

Base Coverage, Cover III

Our base coverage will be COVER III. This coverage separates the field into two areas of deep and short zones. The deep area will be divided into three deep zones—left, right, and middle—called "thirds." The depth of these zones will start at the alignment of the secondary and run the length of the field. The two halfbacks and the safety are responsible for these zones. The short zones will be called "under coverage," and the inside and outside linebackers are responsible for this area. The under coverage will be divided into one middle zone and five zones to each side of the ball. The under coverage has two levels: a top and a bottom. Moving from the ball to the outside, the bottom zones are "hook," "seam," and the "flat" on the outside. On top of the two hook zones is the "hole." Moving from the hole to the outside, the other top zones are the "curl" and the "crease-and-fade" zones. The depth of the bottom level is 10 yards, and the top level is 15 yards from the ball. The size, width, and depth of all zones will change depending on (1) the offensive formation, (2) the number of receivers to a side of a formation, (3) the type of pass routes, and (4) the position of the ball on the field. We will adjust our alignment and coverage zones to these four factors. We will not try to cover the entire field when defending against the pass. Our pass drops will be made only to those zones in which the offense has the capabilities to run routes. We can and will eliminate zones when there is no threat of pass routes in those particular zones.

In order to make the necessary adjustments for pass coverage, we must be able to recognize the passing strength of an offensive formation. It is for this reason that we make a color call after the strength call. The color will identify the receiver set, and also to which side the receivers are aligned. In each offensive formation, we will identify each receiver and his position in the formation by a number.

RECEIVER NUMBERING:

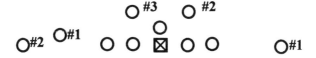

#1 Receiver: First receiver to each side, on or off the line of scrimmage closest to the ball.

#2 Receiver: The next receiver to the outside of #1 receiver on each side, or the nearest back in the backfield.

#3 Receiver: The next receiver to the outside of #2 receiver, or the nearest back in the backfield.

#4 Receiver: The nearest back in the backfield.

(The pass coverage responsibilities for the secondary are explained in Chapter 8. The linebackers' coverage will be described in this chapter.)

THE UNDER COVERAGE FOR LINEBACKERS

The linebackers are responsible for the under coverage, with SAM linebacker responsible for the strongside flat zone. MIKE linebacker has the strongside curl, seam, hook, and hole zones. MEG linebacker has the weakside curl, seam, hook, and hole zones. SARA linebacker has the weakside flat zone. Our pass coverage will be a matchup man-to-man, pattern-read, zone pass defense. This may sound like a lot, but it is really very simple. When the linebackers determine that the play is a pass and they make their pass drop, they should find the receiver in their zone who is aligned closest to the ball (the #1 receiver). If the #1 receiver is running a pass route in his zone, the linebacker must get between him and the quarterback and play man-to-man coverage on him. If the #1 receiver's pass pattern runs to an area which is not the linebacker's coverage area, he should look for either the #2 receiver or the #3 receiver to run a pass route in his zone. If all the receivers to the linebacker's side run pass routes out of his zone, he should pull up and look for receivers from the opposite side running routes in his zone. If nothing shows, he should read the quarterback and break on the ball when it is thrown. When there are two receivers running pass routes in the linebacker's zone, he should cover the deepest one. Before each play, the linebackers must know the receiver alignment and which side is the two-receiver side. When making their pass drop, it is very important that the linebackers know if they are on the one- or two-receiver side. Also, they must know what is the deepest and widest pass route that can be run to their zone from the offensive formation. Once the linebackers determine that the play is a pass, they should start their pass drop. They should aim for the area of their zone where the deepest and widest pass route could be run. Next, they should adjust to the routes run by the receivers. The linebackers should think of the two-receiver side of the offensive formation as the "work" side. The number of receivers and the possibilities for different pass routes will make their job harder. The one-receiver side is the "help" side, because we have two defenders against one receiver and may be able to give help to the two-receiver side. (If the #1 receiver on the two-receiver side runs a crossing pattern, the help side becomes the work side.)

THE ROUTES THAT ARE RUN AT THE TOP OF EACH ZONE ON THE ONE- AND TWO-RECEIVER SIDES

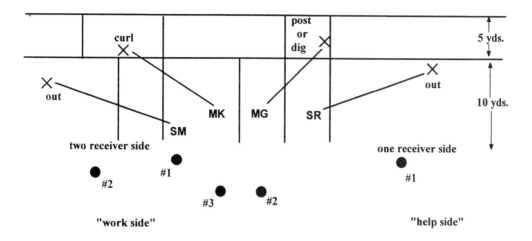

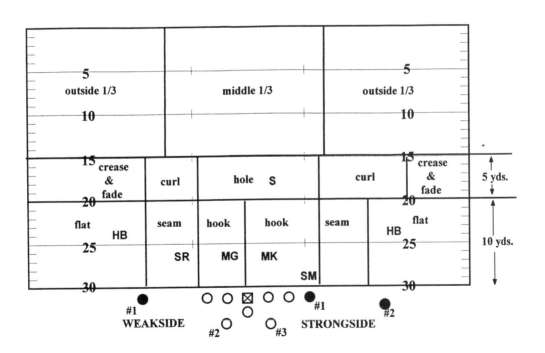

STRONG LEFT BLUE LEFT SPLIT BACKS

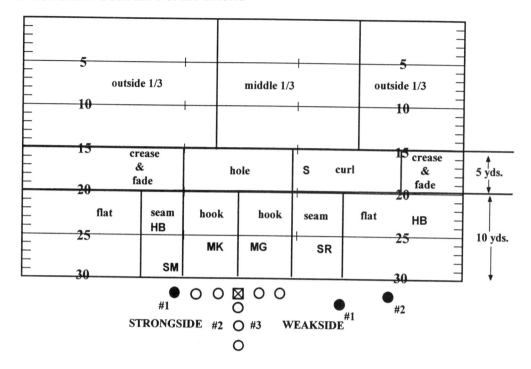

STRONG RIGHT BROWN LEFT "I"

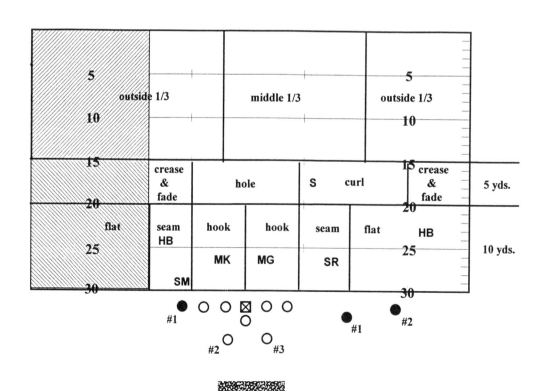

The offensive formation can cut down the size of the field we have to defend. The shaded area represents the area of the field where it would be hard to run more than one pass route. To this side of the formation, we can cut down the width of the pass drops.

UNDER COVERAGE ZONES, RECEIVER ROUTES, AND ROUTES RUN IN ZONES

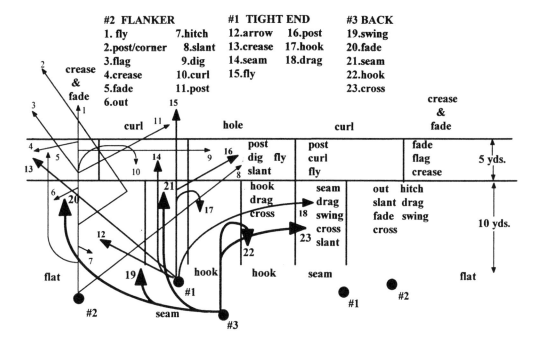

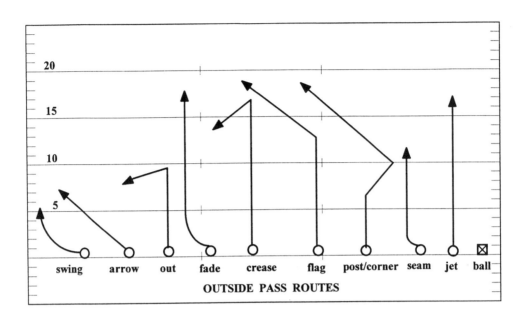

OUTSIDE PASS ROUTES

20

15

10

5

swing arrow out fade crease flag post/corner seam jet ball

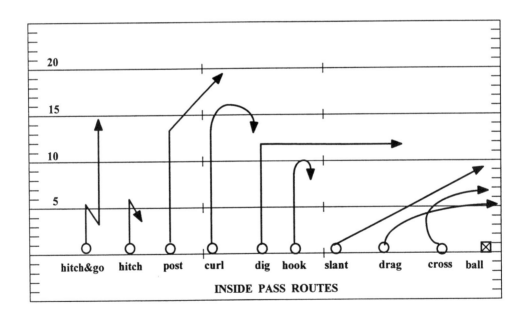

INSIDE PASS ROUTES

20

15

10

5

hitch&go hitch post curl dig hook slant drag cross ball

ALIGNMENT FOR SECONDARY AND LINEBACKER VERSUS RECEIVER SETS

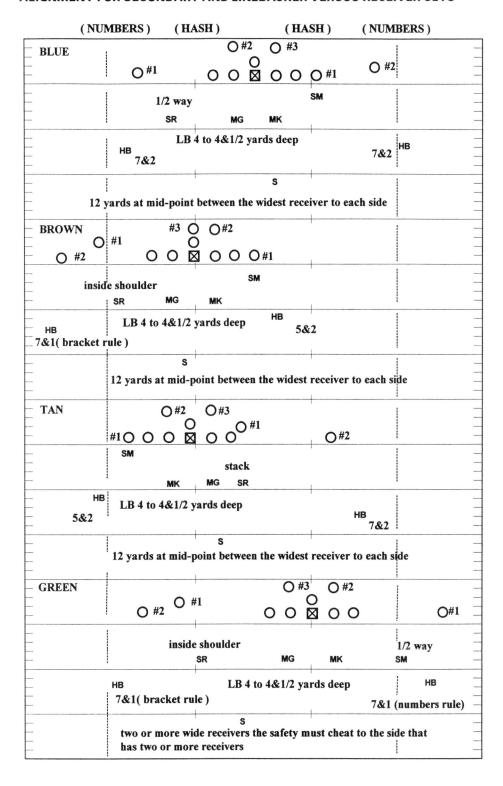

ALIGNMENT FOR SECONDARY AND LINEBACKER VERSUS RECEIVER SETS

(NUMBERS)   (HASH)   (HASH)   (NUMBERS)

BLUE/BROWN

#1   #3
#2   #1   #2

inside shoulder   SM

SR   MG   MK

HB   LB 4 to 4&1/2 yards deep   HB
7&1(bracket rule)   7&2

S
12 yards at mid-point between the widest receiver to each side

BROWN TRIPS

#4   #2
#2   #1
#3   #1

inside shoulder   SM

SR   MG   MK

HB   LB 4 to 4&1/2 yards deep   HB
                                          5&2
7&1(bracket rule)

S
two or more wide receivers the safety must cheat to the side that
has two or more receivers

BLUE TRIPS

#2   #4   #2   #3
#1   #1

1/2 way   over center over tackle inside shoulder
SR   MK   MG   SM

HB   LB 4 to 4&1/2 yards deep   HB
7&1 (numbers rule)   7&1(bracket rule)

S
two or more wide receivers the safety must cheat to the side that
has two or more recrivers

DOUBLE BROWN

#3
#1   #1
#2   #2

inside shoulder   inside shoulder

SR   MG   MK   SM

HB   LB 4 to 4&1/2 yards deep   HB
7&1(bracket rule)   7&1(bracket rule)

S
12 yards at mid-point between the widest receiver to each side

PATTERN READS

The linebackers will use a set order in reading receiver and pass routes, with a slight difference in the way that the inside and the outside linebackers will read those pass routes. The goal of each linebacker is to find and cover the deepest route in his zone. The most efficient way of finding the receiver he should cover is to use a set pattern that puts the receivers in a sequence that is easy to follow.

SAM LINEBACKER: When he is on the two-receiver side, he should first look for the #1 receiver to run a pass route to the flat. If #1 runs a route to another zone, he should continue his pass drop to the flat, looking to the #2 receiver to run a route in his zone. If #2 clears his zone, he should pull up and look for routes coming from the opposite side. If no routes show, he should look for the #3 receiver coming out of the backfield and running routes to the flats. If #3 is not a threat, he should start working back toward the middle. If the Sam linebacker is on the one-receiver side, the #2 receiver will be in the offensive backfield and Sam should look for him to run a route in the flat. He should then look for pass routes coming from the opposite side.

MIKE LINEBACKER: When he is on the two-receiver side, he should first look for the #1 receiver to run a pass route in the seam or hook zone. If the #1 receiver's pass route runs him out of his zone, he should look outside for the #2 receiver to run a post, curl, slant, or dig. If #2 clears his zone, he should look to the opposite side for routes coming to the hole. If nothing shows, he should check for the #3 receiver, who, most of the time, will be a back from the backfield, in the hook or seam. If the Mike linebacker is on the one-receiver side, he should look for the #1 receiver to run a post or dig. If the #1 receiver runs a route out of Mike's zone, he should check for a route to the hole from his opposite side. Next, he should look for the #2 receiver, who, most of the time, will be a back from the backfield, to run a route in the seam or hook.

MEG LINEBACKER: If he is on the two-receiver side, he should first look for the #1 receiver to run a pass route in the curl, seam, or hook zone. If the #1 receiver's pass route runs him out of Meg's zone, he should look outside for the #2 receiver to run a post, curl, slant, or dig. If #2 clears his zone, he should look to the opposite side for routes coming to the hole. If nothing shows, he should check for the #3 receiver, who, most of the time, will be a back from the backfield, in the hook or seam. If the Meg linebacker is on the one-receiver side, he should look for the #1 receiver to run a post or dig. If the #1 receiver runs a route out of his zone, he should check for a route to the hole from the opposite side. Next, he should look for the #2 receiver, most of the time a back from the backfield, to run a route in the seam or hook.

SARA LINEBACKER: If he is on the two-receiver side, he should first look for the #1 receiver to run a pass route to the flat. If #1 runs a route to another zone, Sara should continue his pass drop to the flat, looking to the #2 receiver to run a route in his zone. If #2 clears his zone, he should pull up and look for routes coming from the opposite side. If none show, he should look for the #3 receiver coming out of the backfield and running routes to the flats. If #3 is not a threat, the Sara linebacker should start working back toward the middle. The #2 receiver will be in the offensive backfield, and the Sara linebacker should look for him to run a route in the flat. He should then look for a pass route coming from the opposite side to the flat.

PATTERN READS

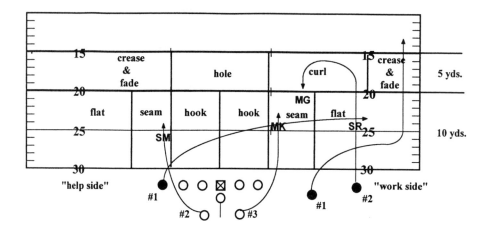

SAM LINEBACKER: Checks #1, calls him across, looks to #2, and covers the seam route.

MIKE LINEBACKER: Checks #1, calls him across, looks to #2 (who's not a threat), looks for routes from the opposite side, sees none, breaks up on #3 coming out of the backfield from the opposite side.

MEG LINEBACKER: Checks #1, sees the fade, looks to #2, sees the curl and covers it.

SARA LINEBACKER: Checks #1, runs with the fade, and looks back and breaks upfield on the drag after running with the fade.

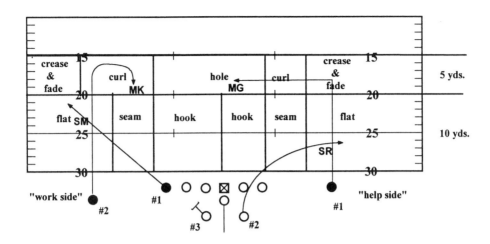

SAM LINEBACKER: Checks #1, sees the arrow and covers it.

MIKE LINEBACKER: Checks #1 (who's not a threat), looks to #2, sees the curl and covers it.

MEG LINEBACKER: Checks #1, plays the dig.

SARA LINEBACKER: Checks #1, slides with the dig, and breaks on #2 in the flat.

WHEN #1 RUNS A ROUTE TO THE OPPOSITE SIDE, THE ONE-RECEIVER SIDE BECOMES THE TWO-RECEIVER SIDE.

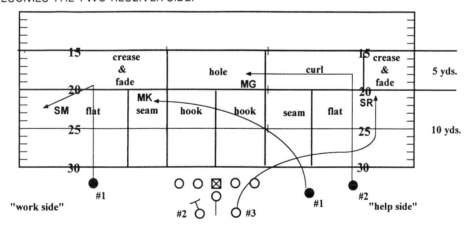

SAM LINEBACKER: Checks #1, gets under the out.

MIKE LINEBACKER: Checks #1 and picks up the drag coming from the opposite side.

MEG LINEBACKER: Checks #1, sees and makes his drop, plays the dig by #1.

SARA LINEBACKER: Checks #1 (who runs out), slides with #2 on the dig, and picks up #3 running the fade.

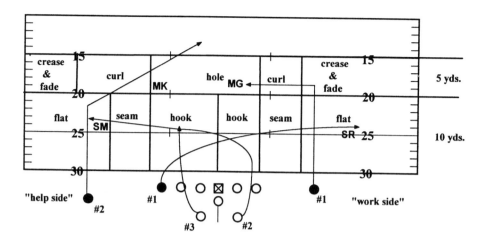

SAM LINEBACKER: Checks #1, calls him across, slides with #2, checks #3, and picks the drag from the opposite-side back.

MIKE LINEBACKER: Checks #1, calls him across, slides with #2 on the post, and breaks up on #3 in the hook zone. (He always plays the deepest route in his zone, and then breaks up the short routes.)

MEG LINEBACKER: Checks #1, plays the dig.

SARA LINEBACKER: Checks #1, slides with the dig and checks #2, picks up the drag from the opposite side.

COVER I ROBBER

Cover I will be used to change our base coverage into an attack coverage. We will be going for the interception or a "Big Hit." The coverage will attack the two-receiver side of the offensive formation and must be run to a two-back set. If the offensive backfield set is ACE, we will check to Cover III. If the offensive play is a running play, we will use our normal FIST III technique. The safety will key the #1 receiver to the two-receiver side and jump the receiver who runs the inside pattern. Keep in mind that we want to go for the interception or the "Big Hit." If the safety reads run action, he should work through the inside receiver to the "alley" to make sure it is not a play-action pass. (Note: If the #1 receiver runs a drag or crossing route to the opposite side, the one-receiver side will become the two-receiver side.)

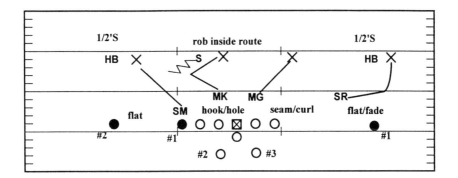

SAFETY: He should align at eight yards deep on the two-receiver side. He should rob the inside pass route to the two-receiver side.

HALFBACKS: They should align head-up the outside receiver, eight yards deep. They are in halves coverage.

SAM LINEBACKER: He uses the normal FIST III technique.

MIKE LINEBACKER: His pass drop will be to the hook zone. He should then open to the opposite side and drop to the hole. He should read the quarterback and look for routes coming in behind the safety. When he is on the one-receiver side, he should use the normal FIST III technique.

MEG LINEBACKER: When he is on the one-receiver side, he should use the normal FIST III technique. When he is on the two-receiver side, his pass drop will be to the hook zone. He should then open to the opposite side and drop to the hole. He should read the quarterback and look for routes coming in behind the safety.

SARA LINEBACKER: If he is on the one-receiver side, he should cheat his alignment a little wider to help play the fade route. In all other situations, he should use the normal technique.

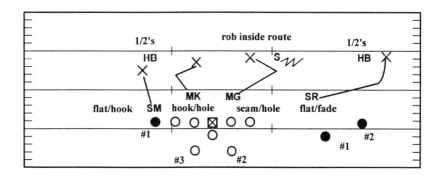

ROBBER TECHNIQUE FOR THE SAFETY

The curl area is the zone in our pass defense that we will rob. It is important that the under coverage sell our opponent that we are not dropping anyone to the curl. We can employ a number of options, including stunting a linebacker or locking the linebacker on any back running a pass route. The safety should use normal FIST III alignment, with the exception of the depth, which should be 8 yards instead of 12 yards. The same pre-snap keys are used to determine run or pass. When pass shows, the safety should pick up the route of the inside receiver (#1), while keying the quarterback's near hand, which is on the ball. While looking for the release of the ball, the safety should open his vision and find the deepest inside route to the two-receiver side. Once the safety has established this route, he should slide and drop, positioning himself on a straight line that runs through the receiver to the hand of the quarterback. When the quarterback drops his near hand off the ball, the safety reads the flight of the ball and breaks on the ball through the receiver. If the receiver's route takes him on a course that will carry him beyond the curl zone, the safety should "man flip" with the receiver, playing under the receiver in man coverage. Whenever possible, the safety should lay back, align, and poise himself for the break on the ball. The safety must be sensitive to two key situations: (1) When the inside receiver (#1) runs a route to the opposite side of the formation (a drag route by the tight end), the safety should slide across with the receiver and rob the curl zone and the inside route on what was the one-receiver side. (2) When the two receivers run short and sideline routes move to the flat and the outside third, with the inside route coming from the one-receiver side (out, flag, and drag), the safety should settle in the curl zone and look for routes coming from the one-receiver side.

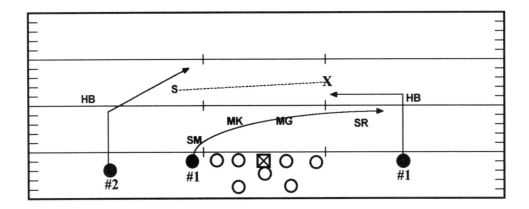

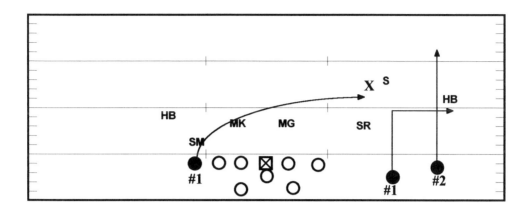

COVER II

Cover II is a run-support coverage. The alignment will be the same as it is with Cover I, with the exception of the safety, whose alignment will be over the center at a depth of eight yards. When the backfield action is "full flow" to a side (all backs going in the same direction), the safety will attack the "alley" toward the full flow. The safety should work through the inside receiver to make sure it is not a play-action pass. He should attack the ball and work from inside out. The halfbacks will read the backs for full flow to a side and drop to halves coverage, looking for either a play-action pass or plays that break. The defensive front will play normal FIST III technique to react to the play. If the backfield action is "split flow" (backs going in different directions) or drop-back pass action, the safety will yell, "Check III!" and everyone will use normal FIST III technique to react to the play.

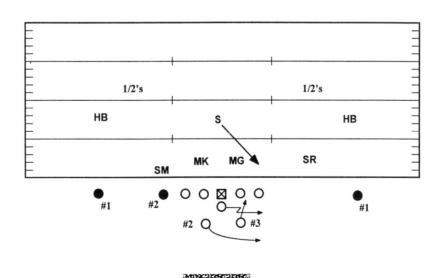

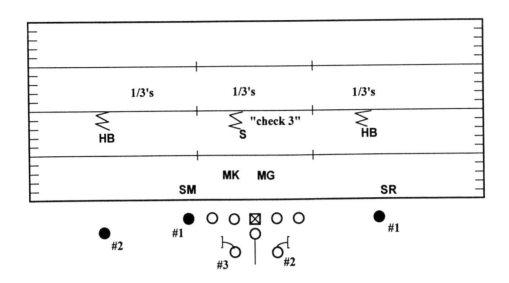

TIGHT FIST III

TIGHT FIST III is a pass coverage we will use during games played in bad weather. When playing in the rain, wind, and cold weather, it is hard to throw the ball to the outside flat area. This defense is designed to cover those areas of high-percentage completion in bad weather.

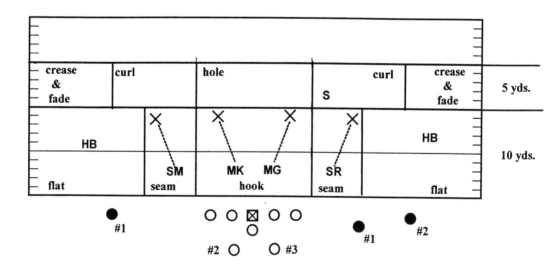

SAM LINEBACKER: He drops to the strongside curl zone, reads the quarterback, breaks on the ball, and traps the receiver.

MIKE LINEBACKER: He drops to the strongside hook zone, reads the quarterback, breaks on the ball, and traps the receiver.

MEG LINEBACKER: He drops to the weakside hook zone, reads the quarterback, breaks on the ball, and traps the receiver.

SARA LINEBACKER: He drops to the weakside curl zone, reads the quarterback, breaks on the ball, and traps the receiver.

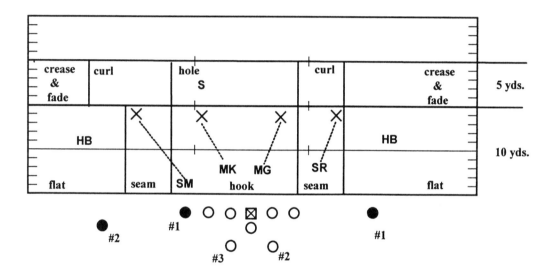

STACK COVER IV

In certain situations, we need to have our best pass defenders on the field. This strategy will require subbing our better pass defender into the game for those linebackers who would be at a disadvantage in certain coverages. The backup safety and the Sara linebacker are the types of players needed to play cover IV. This coverage will be used in situations where we want a four-man pass rush and to still be able to defend against three- or four-deep routes. We will also use this coverage in long-yardage situations. The run/pass keys for the linebackers and the secondary are the same as the ones we use in our base defense, FIST III. The secondary run-support responsibilities are also the same as the ones used in FIST III. The safeties will align to the formation and the field at a depth of 10 yards. Their pass responsibility is the middle fourths of the field. The halfbacks' pass responsibility will be the outside fourths. The halfbacks also help break on and trap routes to the flat. The alignment of the three linebackers will depend on the offensive formation. The outside linebacker's alignment will be, depending on the formation, halfway between the receiver and the offensive tackle, over the inside receiver #1 or #2, or over the offensive tackle, all at a depth of five yards. The run responsibilities are the same as in Stack III for the linebackers, with the middle linebacker responsible for both "A" gaps. When pass shows, the two outside linebackers will drop to the curl zone and then break on routes to the flat. The middle linebacker's alignment will be over the offensive center or tackle, at a depth of five yards, depending on the offensive formation. When pass shows, the middle linebacker will drop to the hole and work to the hook. When making the pass drop, he should open to the side of the formation that presents the most immediate threat to the hook zone. The progression of importance would be (1) the three-receiver side, (2) the two-receiver side, (3) the wide side of the field, (4) the direction in which the ace back steps, and (5) the quarterback's throwing hand. The linebackers' pattern-read techniques will help them identify the most dangerous route to their zone.

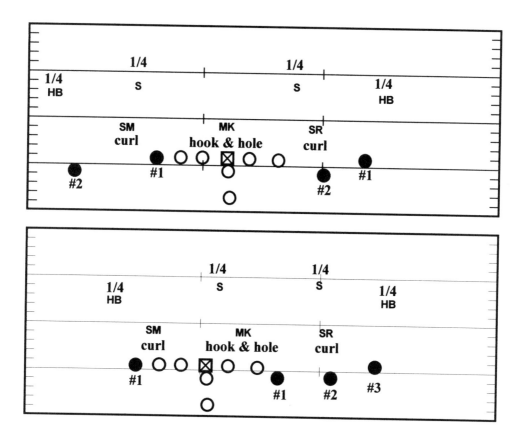

STACK IV COVER I ROBBER

We use this coverage to take advantage of the offense when it tries to attack the curl and flat zones when we are in Cover IV. We need to sell our opponents that we are in Cover IV. Just before the snap, the safeties should move up to a depth of eight yards. The run support is the same as in Cover IV. When pass shows, the outside linebacker will drop to the flats, and the middle linebacker will make the same drop as in Cover IV, playing hook and hole. The halfbacks go to halves coverage and the safeties "rob" the curl zones on both sides, using the same techniques as in Cover I Robber. On the one-receiver side, the safety should key the #1 receiver and the running back to his side. If the offensive formation is a trips set, we will rob only on the trips side. The secondary will check to our normal Cover III, with the one-receiver–side safety in the middle third and the two halfbacks in the outside thirds. Trips will not change the under coverage for either the linebackers, the outside linebacker to the flats, or the middle linebacker to the hook and hole. The trips-side safety should key the middle receiver and rob the curl.

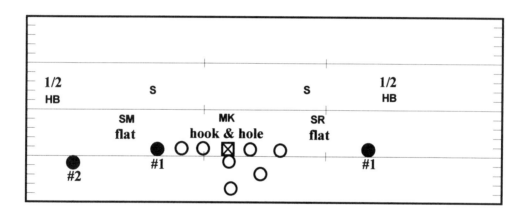

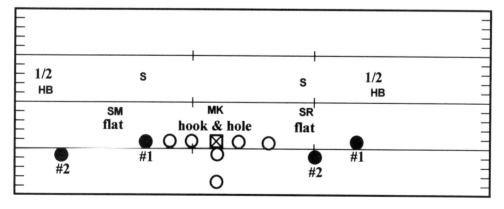

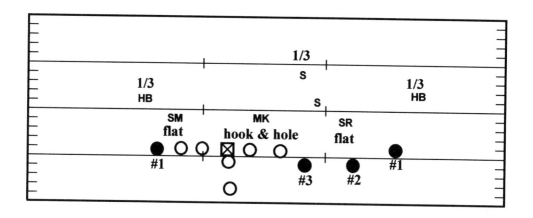

COVER V LOCK

This coverage should not be confused with Cover V or our Nickel coverages. Cover V Lock is another change-up from our Cover IV. We want to show our opponent Cover IV, then just before the snap of the ball, the safeties and halfbacks will move to the coverage. The halfbacks will walk up to the line of scrimmage and lock on in man coverage on the widest receiver to their side. If the widest receiver to a side is a tight end (tan trips, brown), the halfback to the tight end side should move to the opposite side of the offensive formation and align at the safety position. Just before the snap, the halfback moves up to the line of scrimmage, aligning on the second wide receiver from the outside. He should lock on the receiver in man coverage. If any wide receiver to this side goes in motion to the tight end side, the inside halfback runs across the formation with the receiver in man coverage. Just before the snap of the ball, the two safeties will move to the hashes at a depth of 12 yards in halves coverage. The three linebackers will align and play Cover IV technique.

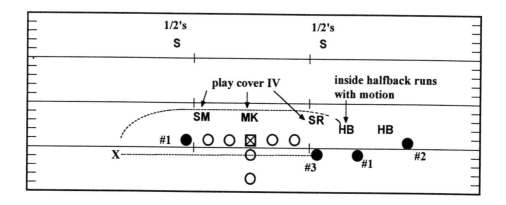

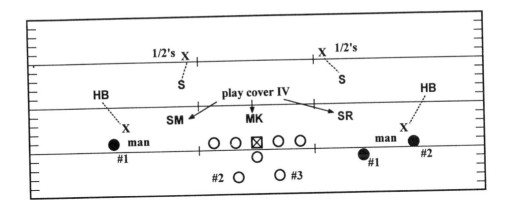

COVER V

Cover V should not be confused with any of our man coverage defenses. We will run Cover V with the personnel we have on the field. It is a five-under zone and two-deep zone defense. We will "roll" up to this coverage as the quarterback is getting under the center. We will run this defense to formations with two or more backs in the backfield. Normally, we will "check" to Cover III to one-back sets; however, we can and will run Cover V to an "ace" backfield set, but only when we have it in our game plan. The safety will make the roll call to the two-receiver side, "roll left, roll left," and the halfback to the two-receiver side will move up to become part of the "under coverage." Anytime the offense sends a receiver in motion, we will roll back to the other side or check to Cover III. When we are in this coverage, we need deep help on the inside receiver (#1) on the two-receiver side and any back out of the backfield running a deep route. Because we are in a two-deep coverage, this coverage will require a linebacker to run deep with the inside pass routes.

OUTSIDE FUNNEL POSITION (FLAT): On the "roll" call, the halfback to the two-receiver side and the outside linebacker to the one-receiver side should move up and out to a position of one yard outside of the widest receiver and four yards deep. The two "funnel" positions will key the near back for a run/pass read; on running plays, they will have "D" gap and #3 on the option. When the play is a pass, they will have the fade and flat. The rolled-up halfback and the outside linebacker on the one-receiver side should use "man" technique with their hands and feet when playing the receiver on pass plays. (See the section of the playbook that covers "man" techniques for the "under coverage.") They should force the receiver to the inside with their hands and feet. They should look through the receiver and stay with him until they see a route coming to the flat from the inside. If the receiver clears their zone, they should keep working to the inside, looking for routes from the inside or opposite side. When the receiver releases outside, they should use "man" technique

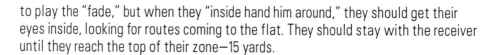

to play the "fade," but when they "inside hand him around," they should get their eyes inside, looking for routes coming to the flat. They should stay with the receiver until they reach the top of their zone—15 yards.

CURL ZONE: The outside linebacker on the two-receiver side will play the curl. He should take his normal FIST III alignment and, on all running plays, use his normal technique. When the play is a pass, he should read the #1 receiver; if he runs any type of deep route, the outside linebacker should use man coverage, wall him off from the inside, and stay with him. The only exception is when the #1 receiver is a tight end or tan back; in that case, the outside linebacker will have inside help. If the #1 receiver releases upfield, the outside linebacker should give him up to the inside linebacker and use his Cover III reads to pick up the next receiver to his zone. If the #1 receiver releases to the flat, he can pick up the next receiver to his zone by using Cover III reads.

HOOK ZONE: The inside linebacker on the two-receiver side will be in a hook zone. He should read the #1 receiver; if he releases upfield, the inside linebacker should wall him off from the inside and stay with him, using man coverage. If the #1 receiver runs a route out of his zone, the inside linebacker should pick up the next receiver to his zone by using Cover III reads. He should keep in mind that, since we have someone in the curl, he doesn't need to make too wide a pass drop.

HOOK-TO-CURL ZONE: The inside linebacker on the one-receiver side will play these zones using Cover III technique to find receivers. The only thing different is that he backs out of the backfield, running deep routes, looking for them and picking them up using man coverage.

HALVES COVERAGE: The halfback and the safety will be 12 yards deep and a yard outside of the hash in halves coverage. They should stay deep and play the pass first. Anytime players have three-deep pass routes, they will have help on the inside receiver. It is important that the halfback and the safety get a good break on the ball. Any miss will result in a touchdown.

COVER V

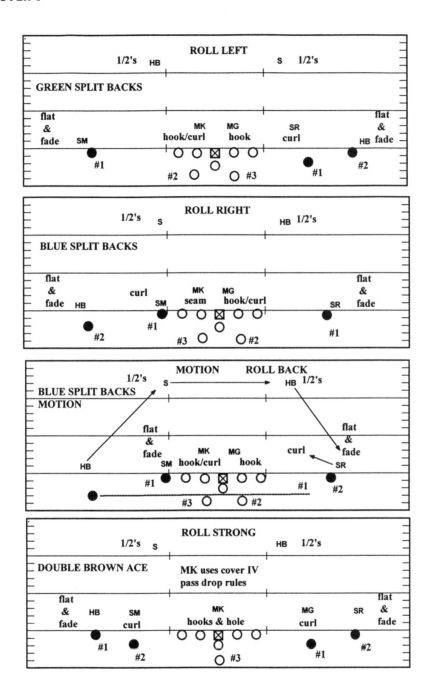

ROLL LEFT

GREEN SPLIT BACKS

ROLL RIGHT

BLUE SPLIT BACKS

MOTION   ROLL BACK

BLUE SPLIT BACKS
MOTION

ROLL STRONG

DOUBLE BROWN ACE   MK uses cover IV
pass drop rules

MAN-TO-MAN (DOG) COVERAGE

This section will deal with our man-to-man coverage defenses. We have three defenses that will incorporate man coverage, NICKEL DOG, PREVENT DOG, and 65 DOG (The word "dog" will refer to man coverage). The alignment and technique for the "under coverage" will be the same for all three coverages. When playing man coverage, good technique will offset any mismatch in speed that we may encounter. However, we must perfect four skills in order to play good man coverage: the alignment, the receiver's release, the trail, and the break on the cut.

ALIGNMENT: When playing man coverage, we must cover every receiver and every back who is eligible for a pass. Although alignment for most offensive formations can be found in this section, if we look at the alignment as adjusting out to the widest receivers, it will make things simple. Also, the number of backs in the backfield will tell us how many receivers we need to adjust to. The halfbacks will always align on the widest receiver. Sam linebacker is the next to adjust out to the receivers, followed by Meg. Mike will always be over a back. Anytime we play man coverage, we want to take away the inside pass route by our alignment. When a receiver or back goes in motion, our defensive players must run with him and also keep their inside position. When covering a receiver who goes in motion, we need to hug the line of scrimmage. When the motion man is going into the formation, we must stay in front of him; when he is going away from the formation, we need to stay behind him. The important thing is to always take away the inside route.

RECEIVER'S RELEASE: The receiver must be made to release to the outside. If the receiver's pattern is to the inside, our defensive players must force him out and around them. In order to accomplish this goal, the defender must use his feet and his hands. Yet his hands and his feet must be used separately. His hands should be used to redirect the receiver to the outside and to knock the receiver off his route. The defender should use his hands the way a boxer does when he throws jabs; he should not commit his feet by trying to throw a knockout punch. The defender should use quick, short steps to front the receiver and guide him to the outside. As the receiver goes around him, the defender should let his inside hand guide him around until he is hip-to-hip with the receiver and heading upfield in the same direction.

THE TRAIL: Once the defender has redirected the receiver and the receiver is running his route, the defender should trail the receiver without trying to catch up with him. A good rule of thumb is for the defender to stay at least two to three yards behind the receiver, and a yard to his inside. If the defender gets too close to the receiver, he will run over the top of the route as soon as the receiver makes his cut. The reason the defender should stay a yard to the inside of the receiver is to enable him to always be in position to be between the receiver and the quarterback.

BREAKING ON THE CUT: When reacting to the receiver's pass cut, the defender has two things going for him: Most pass patterns have only one route cut, and, on average, the quarterback releases the ball on the sixth step of the receiver, after he has made his cut. The defender should trail the receiver and concentrate on his hips. When a receiver makes a cut, two things happen: He shortens his stride, and he drops his hips. When the receiver makes his route cut, the defender should make the same cut at the same time but should not go to the point of the cut to make his break. Next, the defender should make up any lost steps by angling toward the ball, keeping in mind that he has about six steps before the ball will be there. Once the receiver has made his pass cut, the defender should quickly turn his head back toward the ball, looking for the release of the ball by the quarterback. In man fill types of coverages, the defender is taught to watch the hands and the eyes of the receiver so that he knows when to look back and break on the ball. This technique is unnecessary in our man coverage scheme, because the defender will always have deep help (from half coverage players, or in goal line situations when the offense is working in a short field).

MAN-TO-MAN (DOG) COVERAGE

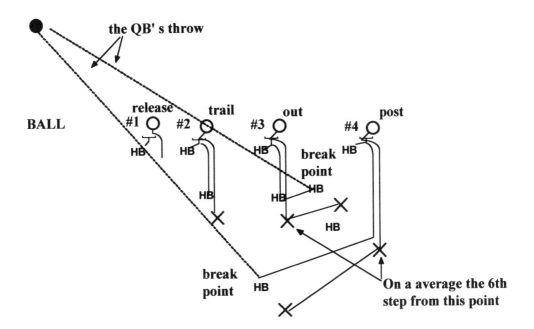

COLLISION POINT, AND TRAILING A BACK RUNNING A ROUTE OUT OF THE BACKFIELD

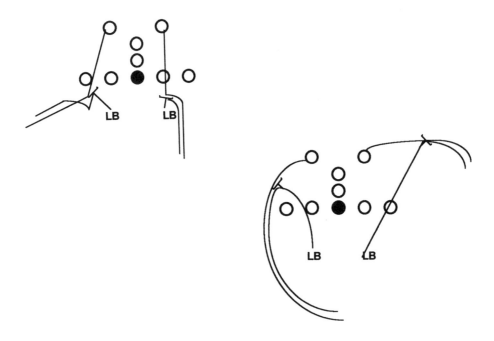

NICKEL DOG

This coverage is a man under two-deep zone defense. The alignment and technique for the "under coverage" used in this defense is the same coverage that's used in our 65 DOG and PREVENT DOG defenses.

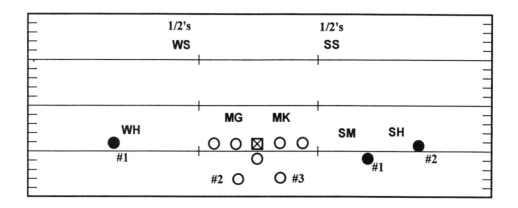

STRONG AND WEAK SAFETIES: They have halves coverage 12 yards deep and one yard outside of the hash.

STRONG AND WEAK HALFBACKS: They have man coverage on the widest receiver to their side.

SAM LINEBACKER: He has man coverage on the tight end. If there is no tight end in the formation, he has man coverage on the middle receiver to the strong side.

MIKE LINEBACKER: He has man coverage on the back to his side. If the backfield set is ace, he has the ace back.

MEG LINEBACKER: He has man coverage on the back to his side. If the backfield set is ace, he has man coverage on the #1 receiver to the weak side or the inside receiver to the trips side.

If our defenders are aligned on any receiver who goes in motion, they should go with him. When they are covering a receiver who goes in motion, they should hug the line of scrimmage. When the motion man is going into the formation, the defenders need to stay in front of him; when he is going away from the formation, they need to stay behind him.

The defensive players must remember to keep inside leverage on the receiver so he doesn't get inside them.

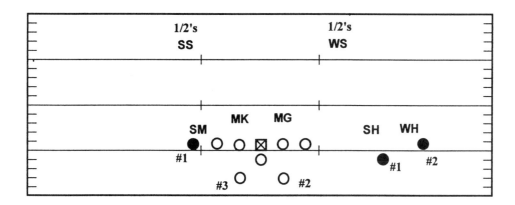

PREVENT ZONE AND PREVENT DOG

SAFETIES 20 YARDS DEEP, THIRDS COVERAGE, AND LINEBACKERS AT SIX YARDS

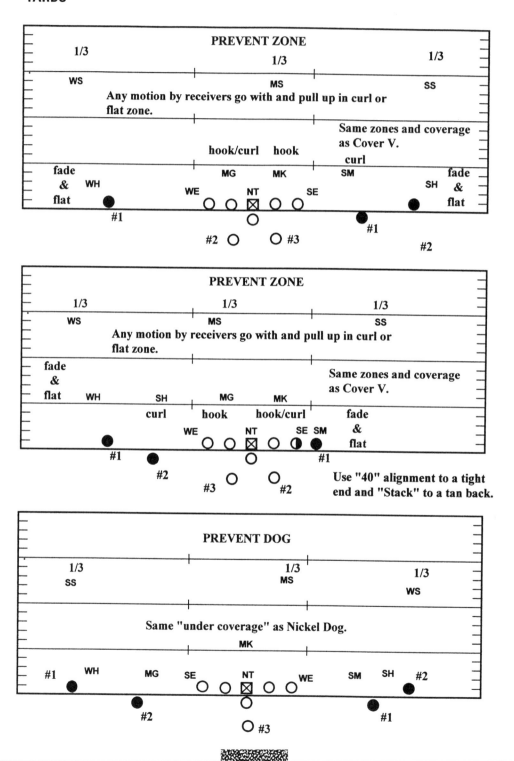

BACKFIELD AND RECEIVER SETS

ALIGNMENT FOR NICKEL, PREVENT, AND 65 DOG

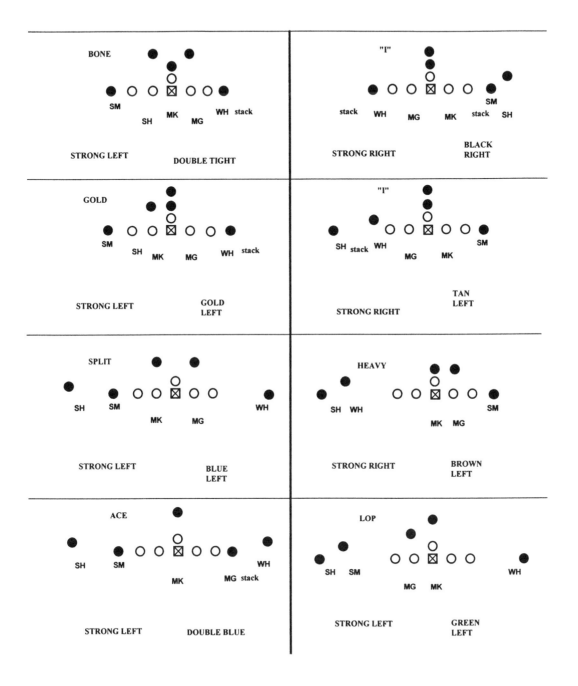

BACKFIELD AND RECEIVER SETS

ALIGNMENT FOR NICKEL, PREVENT, AND 65 DOG

ACE

SH   SM   MG   WH
MK

STRONG RIGHT   DOUBLE BROWN

ACE

SH   stack   SM   MK   MG   stack   WH

STRONG LEFT   DOUBLE TAN

ACE

SH   SM   MG   WH
MK

STRONG LEFT   BLUE/BROWN

ACE

WH   SH   MG   SM
MK

STRONG RIGHT   BROWN TRIPS LEFT

ACE

SM   WH
stack   SH   MK   stack   MG

STRONG LEFT   DOUBLE WING

ACE

SH   MG   SM   WH
MK

STRONG LEFT   BLUE TRIPS LEFT

ACE

SM   WH
SH   stack   MK   MG   stack

S

STRONG LEFT   WING\TAN

ACE

SH   SM   MG   WH
MK

STRONG LEFT   GREEN TRIPS LEFT

CHAPTER 10

Defensive Fronts

STACK

BLUE RIGHT ○ ○ STRONG RIGHT	TAN RIGHT ○ ○ STRONG LEFT

(Defensive alignment diagrams)

BLUE RIGHT — **STRONG RIGHT**
○ ○ ○
○　　　　○ ○ ⊠ ○ ○ ○　　　　○
　　　WE　LT　RT　SE
HB　　SR　　MG　　MK　　SM
　　　　　　　　　S　　　　HB

TAN RIGHT — **STRONG LEFT**
○ ○
○ ○ ○ ⊠ ○ ○　　　　　○
　SE　LT　RT　WE
　　SM　　MK　　MG　　SR
　HB　　　　　S　　　　　HB

BROWN LEFT — **STRONG RIGHT**
○ ○
○　○　　○ ○ ⊠ ○ ○ ○
　　　WE　LT　RT　SE
　　SR　　MG　　MK　　SM
HB　　　　　S　　　　　　HB

GREEN RIGHT — **STRONG LEFT**
○ ○
○ ○ ⊠ ○ ○ ○ ○
○　　SE　LT　RT　WE
　HB　　SM　　MK　　MG　　SR
HB　　　　　　　　S　　　　　HB

STRONG END: He will be in a "switch position" with the Sam linebacker. His alignment will be "stack." If there is a tight end in the game, he should be in a three-point stance over the tight end. In addition, he has "C" gap on running plays and #2 (the quarterback) if the play is an option. If pass shows, the strong end must keep contain on the quarterback.

LEFT TACKLE: He will be in the same alignment as in FIST III.

RIGHT TACKLE: Same as FIST III.

WEAK END: Same as FIST III.

SAM LINEBACKER: This defensive front, Stack III, will put him in a switch position. This alignment will have him a yard outside of the strong end or halfway between the wide receiver and the end lineman on the line of scrimmage at a depth of four to four and a half yards deep. Sam's run responsibility is "D" gap, and he has #3 (the pitch) on the option. His pass coverage is the same as in FIST III: the flat and the seam.

MIKE LINEBACKER: Same as FIST III.

MEG LINEBACKER: Same as FIST III.

SARA LINEBACKER: Same as FIST III.

LEFT HALFBACK: Same as FIST III.

SAFETY: Same as FIST III.

RIGHT HALFBACK: Same as FIST III.

OFFSET

BLUE RIGHT	O O STRONG RIGHT	TAN RIGHT	O O STRONG LEFT

```
BLUE RIGHT     O   O   STRONG RIGHT        TAN RIGHT        O    O     STRONG LEFT
                   O                                             O
  O         O  O ⊠ O O O          O                   O O O ⊠ O O  O          O
        WE  LT    RT  SM SE                        SE SM LT    RT  WE
    SR      MG    MK                                       MK    MG      SR
 HB                          HB                    HB               S              HB
                    S

BROWN LEFT      O   O  STRONG RIGHT        GREEN RIGHT     O    O     STRONG LEFT
                   O                                          O
    O    O    O  O ⊠ O O O                   O         O O ⊠ O O    O    O
         WE   LT    RT  SM SE                     SE  LT   RT  WE
     SR       MG   MK                                 SM   MK   MG     SR
 HB           S             HB              HB                             HB
                                                          S
```

STRONG END: Same as FIST III.

LEFT TACKLE: When the linebacker makes the "shift" call, the left tackle should move quickly to the gap ("A" or "B") toward the strong side. At the snap of the ball, he should penetrate the gap to the heels of the offensive linemen. He should read and react to the play and not get trapped. All else is the same as FIST III.

RIGHT TACKLE: When the linebacker makes the shift call, the right tackle should move quickly to the gap ("A" or "B") toward the strong side. At the snap of the ball, he should penetrate the gap to the heels of the offensive linemen.

He should read and react to the play and not get trapped. All else is the same as FIST III.

WEAK END: Same as FIST III.

SAM LINEBACKER: Same as FIST III.

MIKE LINEBACKER: He makes the shift call and sees to it that the tackles move, and in the right direction. All else is the same as FIST III.

MEG LINEBACKER: He makes sure that Mike makes the shift call. His gap responsibility will change to "B" gap. All else is the same as FIST III.

SARA LINEBACKER: Same as FIST III.

LEFT HALFBACK: Same as FIST III.

SAFETY: Same as FIST III.

RIGHT HALFBACK: Same as FIST III.

"50"

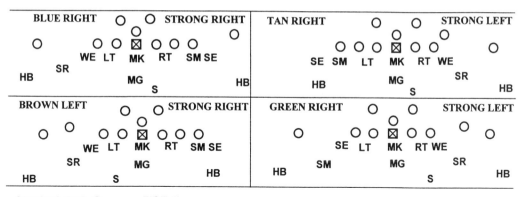

STRONG END: Same as FIST III.

LEFT TACKLE: When the linebacker makes the shift call, the left tackle should move quickly to the "B" gap and align on the outside shoulder of the offensive guard. At the snap, he should come down through the ear of the guard and keep square with the line of scrimmage. He should read and react to the play and not get trapped. All else is the same as FIST III.

RIGHT TACKLE: When the linebacker makes the shift call, the right tackle should move quickly to the "B" gap and align on the outside shoulder of the offensive guard. At the snap, he should come down through the ear of the guard and keep square with the line of scrimmage. He should read and react to the play and not get trapped. All else is the same as FIST III.

WEAK END: Same as FIST III.

SAM LINEBACKER: His duties are the same as in FIST III, except for pass. When the play is a pass, Sam should give up the flat on the one-receiver side and play in the seam and curl zones. On the two-receiver side, he should play the pass the way he does in FIST III.

MIKE LINEBACKER: He makes the shift call and moves to a three-point stance head-up the offensive center. His gap responsibility is both "A" gaps. He should read the helmet of the center, play through the head of the center, and stay square to the line of scrimmage.

MEG LINEBACKER: When Mike makes the shift call, Meg aligns five yards deep over the offensive center. He has no gap or option responsibility and goes to the ball. If the play is a pass, he should play the hook and curl zones to the two-receiver side.

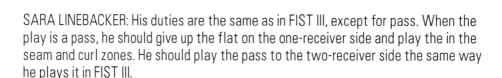

SARA LINEBACKER: His duties are the same as in FIST III, except for pass. When the play is a pass, he should give up the flat on the one-receiver side and play the in the seam and curl zones. He should play the pass to the two-receiver side the same way he plays it in FIST III.

LEFT HALFBACK: Same as FIST III. He must remember that there is no under coverage in the flat on the one-receiver side.

SAFETY: Same as FIST III.

RIGHT HALFBACK: Same as FIST III. He must remember that there is no under coverage in the flat on the one-receiver side.

"40"

WE WILL USE A STACK III ALIGNMENT TO SHIFT OUT OF

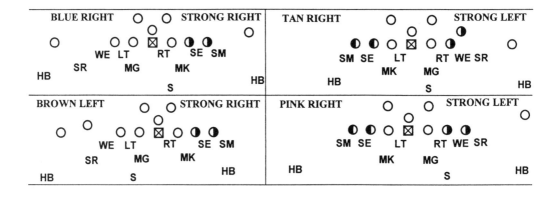

STRONG END: When the Mike linebacker makes the shift call, the strong end should move quickly to a three-point stance, aligning his inside foot on the outside foot of the offensive tackle, crowding the ball. His run responsibility is "C" gap. At the snap, he should penetrate "C" to the hip of the offensive tackle, keep square, and read the play. If option shows, he has #1 to #2 (the dive to the quarterback), whichever shows first. He still has contain on pass plays. When there is no tight end or tan back to his side, he should use his FIST III alignment and responsibilities.

LEFT TACKLE: When Mike makes the shift call, the left tackle should move quickly to the "A" or "B" gap toward the weak side. If his alignment is on the weak side, he should move to the "B" gap; if his alignment is on the strong side, he should move to the "A" gap. At the snap, he should penetrate the gap to the heels of the offensive linemen and read the play. He should make sure not to get trapped.

RIGHT TACKLE: When Mike makes the shift call, the right tackle should move quickly to the "A" or "B" gap toward the weak side. If his alignment is on the weak side, he should move to the "B" gap; if his alignment is on the strong side, he should move to the "A" gap. At the snap, he should penetrate the gap to the heels of the offensive linemen and read the play. He should make sure not to get trapped.

WEAK END: When the Mike linebacker makes the shift call, the weak end should move quickly to a three-point stance, aligning his inside foot on the outside foot of the offensive tackle, crowding the ball. His run responsibility is "C" gap. At the snap, he should penetrate "C" to the hip of the offensive tackle, keep square, and read the play. If option shows, he has #1 to #2 (the dive to the quarterback), whichever shows first. He will still have contain on pass plays. When there is no tight end or tan back to his side, he should use his FIST III alignment and responsibilities.

SAM LINEBACKER: When the Mike linebacker makes the shift call, the Sam linebacker should move quickly to the line of scrimmage. He should align his inside foot on the outside foot of the tight end or the tan back and crowd the ball. His gap responsibility is "D" gap. If the play is an option, he has #2 or #3 (the quarterback or the pitch); his option responsibility will depend on the offensive alignment. If there is no receiver to the outside of his alignment, Sam will have #2 (the quarterback), and the halfback will take #3 (the pitch). If there is a receiver to his outside, he will have #3 (the pitch), and the safety will take #2. If the play is a pass and the player Sam is aligned on blocks down on our end, he should rush the quarterback and keep contain on him. If the tight end or the tan back releases, he should play the pass the same way he does in FIST III. If the offensive alignment has no tight end or tan back, Sam should play everything the same as in FIST III.

MIKE LINEBACKER: He makes the shift call and then moves to the middle of "B" gap four yards deep. His gap responsibility is "B" gap. If the play is an option, he has #1 or #2 (the dive or the quarterback), whichever shows first. He plays the pass the same as he does in FIST III.

MEG LINEBACKER: He plays everything the same way he does in FIST III. The only exception is the option, where he has #1 or #2 (the dive or the quarterback), whichever shows first.

SARA LINEBACKER: If the offensive formation has a tight end or a tan back to his side, the Sara linebacker moves quickly to the line of scrimmage when he hears the shift call from the Mike linebacker. He should align his inside foot to the outside foot of the tight end or the tan back and crowd the ball. His gap responsibility is "D" gap. If the play is an option, Sara has #2 or #3 (the quarterback or the pitch). His option responsibility will depend on the offensive alignment. If there is no receiver to the outside of his alignment, he will have #2 (the quarterback), and the halfback will take #3 (the pitch). If there is a receiver to his outside, the Sara linebacker will have

#3 (the pitch), and the safety will take #2 (the quarterback). If the play is a pass and the player he is aligned on blocks down on our end, Sara should rush the quarterback and keep contain on him. If the tight end or the tan back releases, he should play the pass the same way he does in FIST III. If the offensive alignment has no tight end or tan back, he should play everything the same as FIST III.

LEFT HALFBACK: He has the same responsibilities as in FIST III, with the exception of the option. If the offensive alignment has only a tight end to his side, he will have #3 (the pitch) on option plays. The left halfback must remember to play pass first.

SAFETY: His duties are the same as in FIST III, with the exception of the option, and only when the offensive formation is PINK or BLUE. When the option is run to the two-receiver side, the safety must help cover the option. He should make sure the play is not a pass play, then work through the alley to #2 (the quarterback).

RIGHT HALFBACK: He has the same duties he has in FIST III, with the exception of the option. If the offensive alignment has only a tight end to his side, he will have #3 (pitch) on option plays. The right halfback must remember to play pass first.

"60"

WE WILL USE A STACK III ALIGNMENT TO SHIFT OUT OF

(The only thing different between "40" and "60" is the alignment of the tackles and the Meg linebacker.)

STRONG END: When the Mike linebacker makes the shift call, the strong end should move quickly to a three-point stance, aligning his inside foot on the outside foot of the offensive tackle, crowding the ball. His run responsibility is "C" gap. At the snap, he should penetrate "C" to the hip of the offensive tackle, keep square, and read the play. If option shows, he should have #1 to #2 (the dive to the quarterback), whichever shows first. He will still have contain on pass plays. When there is not tight end or tan back to his side, he should use his FIST III alignment and responsibilities.

LEFT TACKLE: When the Mike linebacker makes the shift call, the left tackle should move quickly to the "A" gap. At the snap, he should penetrate the gap to the heels of the offensive linemen and react to the play. He should make sure he doesn't get trapped.

RIGHT TACKLE: When the Mike linebacker makes the shift call, the right tackle should move quickly to the "A" gap. At the snap, he should penetrate the gap to the heels of the offensive linemen and react to the play. He should make sure he doesn't get trapped.

WEAK END: When the Mike linebacker makes the shift call, the weak end should move quickly to a three-point stance, aligning his inside foot on the outside foot of the offensive tackle, crowding the ball. His run responsibility is "C" gap. At the snap, he should penetrate "C" to the hip of the offensive tackle, keep square, and read the play. If option shows, he has #1 to #2 (the dive to the quarterback), whichever shows first. He will still have contain on pass plays. When there is no tight end or tan back to his side, he should use his FIST III alignment and responsibilities.

SAM LINEBACKER: When the Mike linebacker makes the shift call, the Sam linebacker should move quickly to the line of scrimmage. He should align his inside foot on the outside foot of the tight end or the tan back, crowding the ball. His gap responsibility is "D" gap. If the play is an option, he has #2 or #3 (the quarterback or the pitch). His option responsibility will depend on the offensive alignment. If there is no receiver to the outside of his alignment, he will have #2 (the quarterback), and the halfback will take #3 (the pitch). If there is a receiver to his outside, he will have #3 (the pitch), and the safety will take #2 (the quarterback). If the play is a pass, and the player Sam is aligned on blocks down on our end, he should rush the quarterback and keep contain on him. If the tight end or the tan back releases, Sam should play the pass the same way he does in FIST III. If the offensive alignment has no tight end or tan back, he should play everything the same as in FIST III.

MIKE LINEBACKER: He makes the shift call and moves to the middle of "B" gap four yards deep. His gap responsibility is "B" gap. If the play is an option, he has #1 or #2 (the dive or the quarterback), whichever shows first. He plays the pass the same as he does in FIST III.

MEG LINEBACKER: When the Mike linebacker makes the shift call, Meg moves to the middle of gap "B" at a depth of four yards. His gap responsibility is "B" gap. If the play is an option, he has #1 or #2 (the dive or the quarterback), whichever shows first. He should play the pass the same as he does in FIST III.

SARA LINEBACKER: If the offensive formation has a tight end or a tan back to his side, the Sara linebacker should move quickly to the line of scrimmage on the shift call from the Mike linebacker. He should align his inside foot on the outside foot of the tight end or the tan back, crowding the ball. His gap responsibility is "D" gap. If the play is an option, the Sara linebacker has #2 or #3 (the quarterback or the pitch). His option responsibility will depend on the offensive alignment. If there is no receiver to the outside of his alignment, Sara will have #2 (the quarterback), and the halfback will take #3 (the pitch). If there is a receiver to his outside, he will have #3 (the pitch), and the safety will take #2 (the quarterback). If the play is a pass, and the player Sara is aligned on blocks down on our end, he should rush the quarterback and keep contain on him. If the tight end or the tan back releases, he should play the pass the same way he does in FIST III. If the offensive alignment has no tight end or tan back, the Sara linebacker should play everything the way he does in FIST III.

GOAL LINE DEFENSE

65 DOG

When we are in our Goal Line Defense, 65 DOG, we must remember to do three things: (1) Make sure we have the proper alignment. (2) Take care of our responsibility. (3) Stay low (low man wins) and sell out to the ball. There is no tomorrow—mistakes, hesitation, indecision all mean touchdown.

Strength: We will call strength to the tight end. If there are two tight ends, the strength will be to the two-receiver side. If there are no tight ends, the strength will be to the two-receiver side. It is very important that we know what the backfield set is. The strength call will be made by the SAM and MIKE linebackers.

Alignment: The alignment for the down linemen is very simple. The alignment for linebackers and halfbacks is also simple, if they follow some basic rules. Defenders should never align in the end zone or let a receiver get inside of them.

Responsibility: There are only three things to think about: run (gap), option, and pass.

LEFT AND RIGHT GUARDS: They should both align on the inside shoulder of the offensive guard, with their outside foot on the inside foot of the guard. They have "A" gap; at the snap, they come hard through the hip of the offensive center. They should stay low and keep from being trapped. They have #1 on the option and the inside pass rush.

LEFT AND RIGHT TACKLES: They should align on the outside shoulder of the tackle, with their inside foot on the outside foot of the offensive tackle. The tackles have

"C" gap. At the snap, they should get under the pads of the offensive tackle, stay low, and keep from getting trapped. They have #1 to #2 on option plays, but if the tackle blocks down and the ball is in level one, they have #1. If the tackle blocks out on them and the ball is in level one, they have #2. When the play is a pass, they should rush the passer, but do it on the inside, coming under the tackle. The only time their alignment will change is when there is an ace back and no tight end. When the backfield set is ace, they will "reduce," which will move them to the middle of "B" gap.

STRONG END: He plays everything the same as in FIST III, with "D" gap, #3 on option plays, and contain on the quarterback. He must keep in mind, however, that the most used misdirection plays at the goal line are bootlegs. If the play goes to the opposite side, the strong end should not pursue until he is certain it is not a bootleg, a reverse, or a broken play.

WEAK END: He uses a stack alignment on a tight end or a tan back and the FIST alignment to an open formation. When there is a tight end or a tan back, the weak end should read his block. If the tight end or the tan back blocks down, the weak end should come hard to the inside to whoever has the ball. If the tight end or the tan back blocks him or releases, then the weak end has "D" gap, #3 on the option, and contain on the quarterback. If the formation is open (no tight end or tan back), his play is the same: #3, "D" gap, and contain. He should keep in mind, however, that the most used misdirection plays at the goal line are bootlegs. If the play goes to the opposite side, the weak end should not pursue until he is certain it is not a bootleg, a reverse, or a broken play.

The alignment for the linebackers and the halfbacks can be confusing if the coach allows it to be confusing. The important point to keep in mind is that our defenders need to cover all the backs and eligible receivers. They should never align in the end zone. When a back or a receiver goes in motion, someone has to run with him. It is imperative, therefore, that the defenders know how many backs are in the backfield and to which side is the strength. All these things will help our defense get aligned properly.

MIKE LINEBACKER: He will be in the middle, and his alignment will be over the running back on the strong side. He has the "B" gap on run plays and #1 to #2 on option plays. His key is the near back, and he should work from the inside to the outside, taking what shows first. He should play man coverage on the first back out to his side. If the play is a pass and the backs pass block, Mike should make a pass drop and then look inside for crossing routes.

MEG LINEBACKER: When there are two or more backs in the backfield, he will align over the back to the weak side. He has "B" gap on run plays and #1 to #2 on option plays. His key is the near back, and he should work from the inside to the outside, taking what shows first. He should play man coverage on the first back out to his side. If the play is a pass, and the backs pass block, Meg should make a pass drop and look inside for crossing routes. If any back goes in motion, the Meg linebacker must go with him and cover him using man technique. If the backfield set is ace, the Meg linebacker must adjust out to the inside receiver on the side that has two or more receivers.

SAM LINEBACKER: Sam's first responsibility is pass, followed by run. His alignment will be over the tight end anytime there is one in the game. He should take away the inside cut and play the run if the tight end blocks. If there is no tight end in the game, Sam should align to the inside of the middle receiver on the side that has two or more receivers.

STRONG HALFBACK: His responsibility is pass, pass, and then run. He should check the backfield set. If there are three backs, his alignment is in the middle over a back. If any back goes in motion, he should take him. If the play is a run, he should go to the ball. When there are two or fewer backs in the backfield, he should align inside of the widest receiver to the strong side. He should take away the inside route by his alignment. He should play under and to the inside of the pass route. The Sam linebacker and the strong halfback should almost always be to the same side. An important note is that the only time both halfbacks will be on the same side is TAN, TAN TRIPS, BROWN, and BROWN TRIPS. When the strong halfback's alignment is a stack behind the weak end (TAN and BLACK are the only times), he should take away the inside route by his alignment. He should play pass first, cut off the inside route, and get under the receiver. (If the tan back blocks down, the strong halfback should fill outside his block, taking "D" gap and #3 on option plays.) If the tan back tries to "reach block" the weak end, the strong halfback should fill inside and go to the ball.

WEAK HALFBACK: His responsibility is pass, pass, and then run. His alignment will always be to the weak side on the widest receiver. He should take away the inside route by his alignment. He should play under and to the inside of the pass route. If the widest receiver is a tight end, then the weak halfback's alignment will be in a stack behind the weak end. He should take away the inside by his alignment. He should play pass first, cut off the inside route, and get under the receiver. If the tight end blocks down, he should fill outside his block, taking "D" gap and #3 on option plays. If the end tries to "reach block" the weak end, the weak halfback should fill inside and go to the ball. The weak end and the weak halfback will always be to the same side.

BACKFIELD AND RECEIVER SETS AND ALIGNMENT FOR 65 DOG

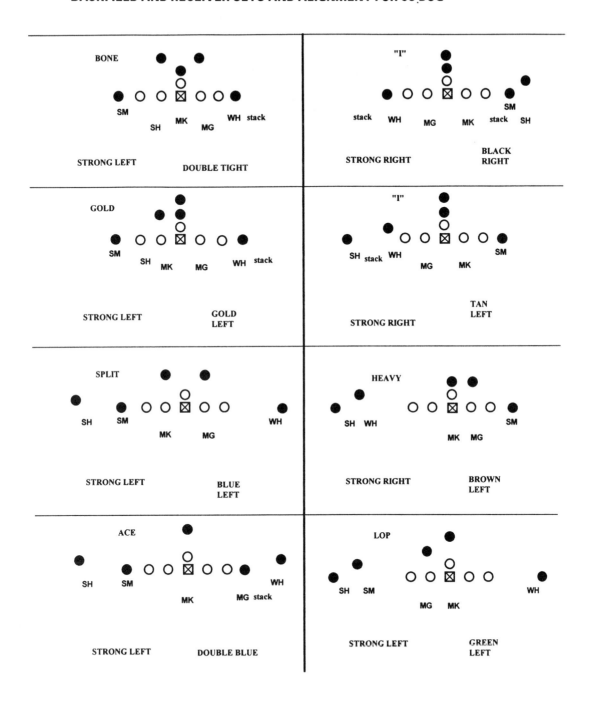

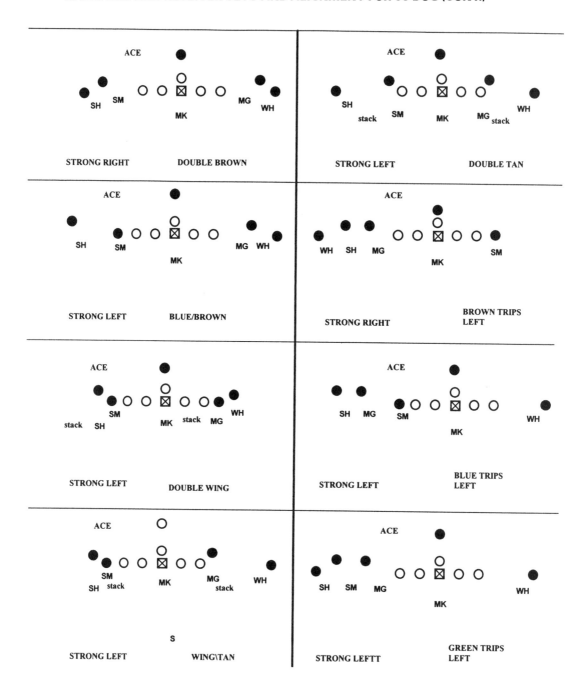

STRONG RIGHT — DOUBLE BROWN

STRONG LEFT — DOUBLE TAN

STRONG LEFT — BLUE/BROWN

STRONG RIGHT — BROWN TRIPS LEFT

STRONG LEFT — DOUBLE WING

STRONG LEFT — BLUE TRIPS LEFT

STRONG LEFT — WING\TAN

STRONG LEFTT — GREEN TRIPS LEFT

CHAPTER 11

Stunts

The purpose of the stunt is to create and force turnovers, interceptions, big plays, sacks, and hurries. When running a stunt, we want to put pressure on the offense, at little or no risk to the defense. To accomplish this we must know our alignment, responsibilities, and coverage of any type of offensive play. If we have to give up something to gain something, then let it be something that has a low-percentage rate of completion and will not result in a touchdown. Ensuring low risk will require the defense to communicate and play together. Each player must know his run support, option, and pass responsibilities. The linebackers and the secondary must know what zones we are giving up in our "under coverage." Each position must know how the stunt will affect the play of their position and the defense as a unit! We cannot have a member of the defensive front say to himself, "The stunt is to the opposite side, it does not affect me," or the secondary say, "We don't change our coverage when we stunt, so it doesn't affect my play." When we stunt, we are changing the attack of our defense, which will cause the offense to react differently to our defense. On each stunt, we must know and communicate run, option, and pass responsibilities. The front and the linebackers must communicate with each other—who has contain, who has what gap, and who is responsible for #1, #2, or #3 on the option. The linebackers must communicate with each other about who is covering what zone ("You're going, I've got the seam"). The linebackers must tell the secondary which area of the under coverage will not be covered.

PASS COVERAGE FOR STUNTS

When we stunt, the shaded zones will always have under coverage. A linebacker will be responsible for these zones.

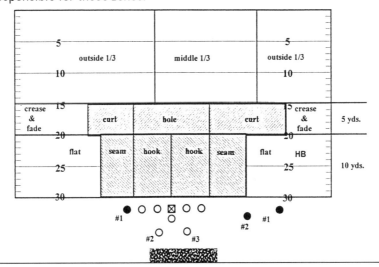

WHEN WE RUN A STUNT WHICH INVOLVES THE OUTSIDE LINEBACKERS (SAM AND SARA), THE HALFBACK TO THE OPEN FIELD SHOULD CHEAT HIS ALIGNMENT TO HEAD-UP OR A YARD INSIDE OF THE WIDE RECEIVER, DEPENDING ON THE DISTANCE OF THE SPLIT.

INSIDE STUNTS

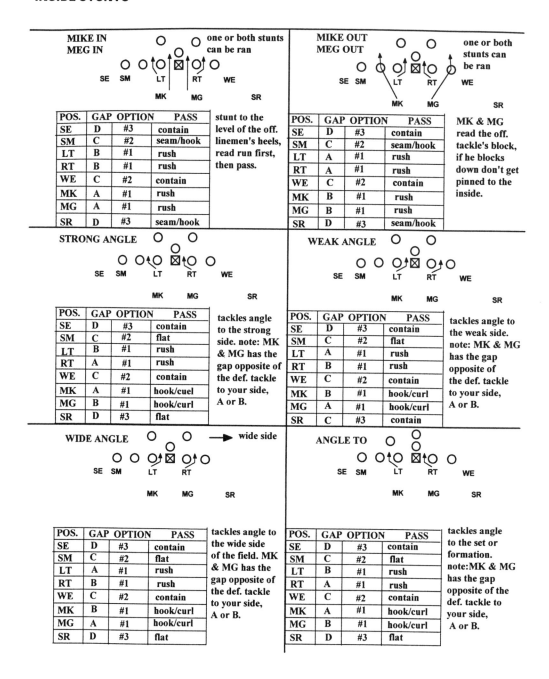

MIKE IN / MEG IN — one or both stunts can be ran

POS.	GAP	OPTION	PASS
SE	D	#3	contain
SM	C	#2	seam/hook
LT	B	#1	rush
RT	B	#1	rush
WE	C	#2	contain
MK	A	#1	rush
MG	A	#1	rush
SR	D	#3	seam/hook

stunt to the level of the off. linemen's heels, read run first, then pass.

MIKE OUT / MEG OUT — one or both stunts can be ran

POS.	GAP	OPTION	PASS
SE	D	#3	contain
SM	C	#2	seam/hook
LT	A	#1	rush
RT	A	#1	rush
WE	C	#2	contain
MK	B	#1	rush
MG	B	#1	rush
SR	D	#3	seam/hook

MK & MG read the off. tackle's block, if he blocks down don't get pinned to the inside.

STRONG ANGLE

POS.	GAP	OPTION	PASS
SE	D	#3	contain
SM	C	#2	flat
LT	B	#1	rush
RT	A	#1	rush
WE	C	#2	contain
MK	A	#1	hook/cuel
MG	B	#1	hook/curl
SR	D	#3	flat

tackles angle to the strong side. note: MK & MG has the gap opposite of the def. tackle to your side, A or B.

WEAK ANGLE

POS.	GAP	OPTION	PASS
SE	D	#3	contain
SM	C	#2	flat
LT	A	#1	rush
RT	B	#1	rush
WE	C	#2	contain
MK	B	#1	hook/curl
MG	A	#1	hook/curl
SR	C	#3	contain

tackles angle to the weak side. note: MK & MG has the gap opposite of the def. tackle to your side, A or B.

WIDE ANGLE — wide side

POS.	GAP	OPTION	PASS
SE	D	#3	contain
SM	C	#2	flat
LT	A	#1	rush
RT	B	#1	rush
WE	C	#2	contain
MK	B	#1	hook/curl
MG	A	#1	hook/curl
SR	D	#3	flat

tackles angle to the wide side of the field. MK & MG has the gap opposite of the def. tackle to your side, A or B.

ANGLE TO

POS.	GAP	OPTION	PASS
SE	D	#3	contain
SM	C	#2	flat
LT	B	#1	rush
RT	A	#1	rush
WE	C	#2	contain
MK	A	#1	hook/curl
MG	B	#1	hook/curl
SR	D	#3	flat

tackles angle to the set or formation. note:MK & MG has the gap opposite of the def. tackle to your side, A or B.

STRONGSIDE AND WEAKSIDE OUTSIDE STUNTS

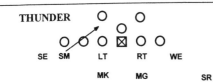

THUNDER

SE SM   LT   RT   WE
MK   MG   SR

POS.	GAP	OPTION	PASS
SE	D	#3	contain
SM	C	#2	inside rush
LT	B	#1	rush
RT	B	#1	rush
WE	C	#2	contain
MK	A	#1	hook/curl
MG	A	#1	hook/curl
SR	D	#3	flat

the aim point for SM is the hip of the off. tackle. you have inside pass rush come under the pass blocks by backs and linemen.

THUNDER (from a "switch" position)

SM SE   LT   RT   WE
SM   MK   MG   SR

POS.	GAP	OPTION	PASS
SE	C	#2	inside rush
SM	D	#3	contain
LT	B	#1	rush
RT	B	#1	rush
WE	C	#2	contain
MK	A	#1	hook/curl
MG	A	#1	hook/curl
SR	D	#3	flat

the aim point for SM is the outside shoulder of the deepest back. strong end has inside pass rush come under the pass blocks by backs & linemen.

SCISSOR

SE—SM   LT   RT   WE
MK   MG   SR

("RED" to a "switch" call)

POS.	GAP	OPTION	PASS
SE	C	#2	inside/rush
SM	D	#3	contain
LT	B	#1	rush
RT	B	#1	rush
WE	C	#2	contain
MK	A	#1	hook/curl
MG	A	#1	hook/curl
SR	D	#3	flat

SM step to the outside, strong end come behind and square up. the end has inside pass rush come under the pass blocks by backs & linemen.

HOT
("RED" if two wide rec. to your side)

SE SM   LT   RT   WE SR
MK   MG   SR

POS.	GAP	OPTION	PASS
SE	D	#3	flat
SM	C	#2	contain
LT	B	#1	rush
RT	B	#1	rush
WE	C	#2	inside rush
MK	A	#1	hook/curl
MG	A	#1	hook/curl
SR	D	#3	contain

the aim point for SR is the outside shoulder of the deepest back. weak end has inside pass rush come under the pass blocks by backs & linemen.

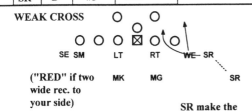

WEAK CROSS

SE SM   LT   RT   WE SR
("RED" if two wide rec. to your side)   MK   MG   SR

POS.	GAP	OPTION	PASS
SE	D	#3	contain
SM	C	#2	flat
LT	B	#1	rush
RT	A	#1	rush
WE	D	#3	contain
MK	A	#1	hook/curl
MG	C	#2	hook/curl
SR	B	#1	inside rush

SR make the stunt look like a "HOT". go behind the weak end through "B" gap. SR has inside pass rush, come under the pass blocks of backs and linemen.

MEG OUT FLY

SE SM   LT   RT   WE MG
MK   MG   SR

POS.	GAP	OPTION	PASS
SE	D	#3	contain
SM	C	#2	flat
LT	B	#1	rush
RT	A	#1	rush
WE	B	#1	inside rush
MK	A	#1	hook/curl
MG	C	#2	contain
SR	D	#3	seam/hook

weak end read the off. tackle, if the tackle blocks down, come off his hip, blocks out come under. MG aim point is the outside shoulder of the deepest back.

READ STUNTS

When we run "read stunts," the idea is to choose our attack of an offensive play on the basis of how that play is being blocked. The positions involved in the stunt will react and determine their path to the ball by keying a predetermined offensive player's block or release.

STRONG SQUEEZE

The tackle on the strong side, the strong end, the Sam linebacker, and the Mike linebacker will all run the strong squeeze stunt. If the offensive formation does not have a tight end but does have a tan back to the strong side, the stunt will be run from the "switch position," with the end and the Sam linebacker exchanging responsibilities. If the formation has neither a tight end nor a tan back to the strong side, the defense will either "RED" out of the stunt or change the stunt to strong Sally. We will give up the flat to the strong side.

STRONGSIDE TACKLE: He stunts to the "A" gap, using the same technique as Mike or Meg Out.

SAM LINEBACKER: His gap responsibility will be "B" or "C"; his option responsibility will be #1 or #2, depending on the block of the offensive tackle. At the snap, he should step down hard through the ear of the offensive tackle. If the tackle turns out to block him, Sam should get under his pads, square up to the line of scrimmage, constrict "B" gap, and play "C" gap and #2 on the option. If the tackle blocks down or releases downfield, Sam should close it down to "B" gap and #1 on option plays. He should keep outside leverage on any blocks coming from the inside, the fullback, or the guard trying to kick him out. If the tackle pass blocks, Sam has an inside pass rush.

STRONG END: His gap responsibility will be "C" or "D," plus #2 or #3 on option plays, depending on the release or block of the tight end. At the snap, the strong end should step down hard through the ear of the tight end. If the end turns out to block him, the strong end should get under his pads, square up to the line of scrimmage, constrict "C" gap, and play "D" gap and #3 on the option. If the end blocks down or releases downfield, the strong end should close it down to "C" gap and #2 on option plays. He should keep outside leverage on any blocks coming from the inside, the fullback, or the guard trying to kick him out. If the play is a pass, the end has contain on the quarterback.

MIKE LINEBACKER: The Mike linebacker should use his normal keys. When his key takes him to the strong side, Mike should pick up the offensive tackle's block. If he is blocking out on the Sam linebacker, Mike should come hard to "B" gap, keep outside leverage on all blocks, and make the play. Mike has "B" gap and #1 on the option. If the tackle comes out on him, Mike should take him on head-up and bounce it out to

"D" gap and #3 on the option. If the play is pass, Mike should check the tight end and drop to the seam and hook. If the play is to the weak side, he should play it as he would in FIST III.

TEAR

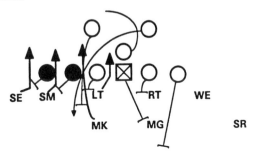

TACKLE: Stunt "A" gap

SAM LINEBACKER: Square up, "C" gap

STRONG END: Square up, "D" gap

MIKE LINEBACKER: Bust "B" gap

OPTION

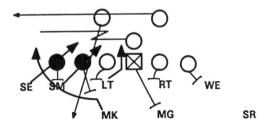

TACKLE: Stunt "A" gap, #1 option

SAM LINEBACKER: Go hard through the hip of the tackle "B" gap, #1 on the option

STRONG END: Go hard through the hip of the end "C" gap, #2 on the option

MIKE LINEBACKER: Take the tackle on straight up and bounce to "D" gap, #3 on the option

POWER

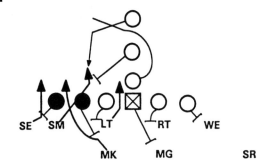

TACKLE: Stunt "A" gap

SAM LINEBACKER: Go hard through the hip of the tackle "B" gap; keep outside leverage on the fullback

STRONG END: Square up, "D" gap

MIKE LINEBACKER: Take the tackle on straight up and bounce to "C"

SPRINT PASS

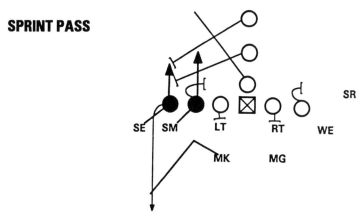

TACKLE: Stunt "A" gap; pass rush

SAM LINEBACKER: Go hard through the hip of the tackle "B"; inside pass rush

STRONG END: Pass rush; contain the quarterback

MIKE LINEBACKER: Read pass, check the tight end, seam and hook

WEAK SQUEEZE

We will run weak squeeze only to a two-tight end set or a tan set. To any other offensive set, we will "red" out of the stunt or change the stunt to weak Sally. The weakside tackle, the weak end, the Sara linebacker, and the Meg linebacker will run the weak squeeze stunt.

WEAKSIDE TACKLE: He stunts to "A" gap and uses the same technique as Mike or Meg Out.

WEAK END: He keys the offensive tackle for his movement. The weak end's gap responsibility will be "B" or "C," and #1 or #2 on the option, depending on the block of the offensive tackle. At the snap, the weak end should step down hard through the ear of the offensive tackle. If the tackle turns out to block him, the weak end should get under his pads, square up to the line of scrimmage, constrict "B" gap, and play "C" gap and #2 on the option. If the tackle blocks down or releases downfield, the weak end should close it down to "B" gap, and #1 on option plays. He should keep outside leverage on any blocks coming from the inside, the fullback, or the guard trying to kick him out. If the tackle pass blocks, he has inside pass rush.

SARA LINEBACKER: Just before the snap, he moves up to the line of scrimmage, outside of the weak end. He should key either the tight end or the tan back for his movement. The Sara linebacker's gap responsibility will be "C" or "D," and #2 or #3 on option plays, depending on the release or the block of the tight end or tan back. At the snap, the Sara linebacker should step down hard through the ear of the tight end or the tan back. If the end or the tan back turns out to block him, Sara should get under his pads, square up to the line of scrimmage, constrict "C" gap, and play "D" gap and #3 on the option. If the end or the tan back blocks down or releases downfield, Sara should close it down to "C" gap, and #2 on option plays. He should keep outside leverage on any blocks coming from the inside, the fullback, or the guard trying to kick him out. If the play is a pass, the Sara linebacker has contain on the quarterback.

MEG LINEBACKER: The Meg linebacker should use his normal keys. When his key takes him to the weak side, Meg should pick up the offensive tackle's block. If he is blocking out on the weak end, he should come hard to "B" gap. He should keep outside leverage on all blocks and make the play; he has "B" gap and #1 on the option. If the tackle comes out on him, Meg should take him on head-up and bounce it out to "D" gap; he has #3 on option plays. If the play is pass, he should check the tight end (or tan back) and drop to the seam and hook. If the play is to the strong side, he should play it as he would in FIST III.

WEAK SQUEEZE

TEAR

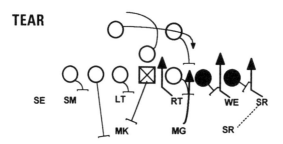

TACKLE: Stunt "A" gap

WEAK END: Square up, "C" gap

SARA LINEBACKER: Square up, "D" gap

MEG LINEBACKER: Bust "B" gap

OPTION

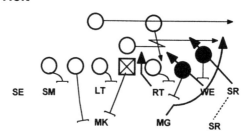

TACKLE: Stunt "A" gap, #1 option

WEAK END: Go hard through the hip of the tackle "B" gap, #1 on the option

SARA LINEBACKER: Go hard through the hip of the tan back "C" gap, #2 on the option

MEG LINEBACKER: Take the tackle on straight up and bounce to "D" gap, #3 on the option

POWER

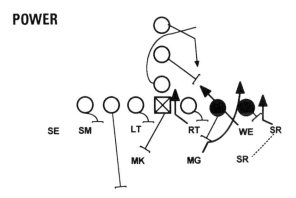

TACKLE: Stunt "A" gap

WEAK END: Go hard through the hip of the tackle "B" gap, keep outside leverage on the fullback

MEG LINEBACKER: Take the tackle on straight up and bounce to "C"

SPRINT PASS

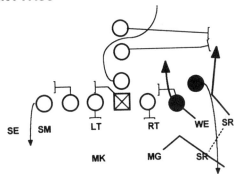

TACKLE: Stunt "A" gap, pass rush

WEAK END: Go hard through the hip of the tackle "B," inside pass rush

SARA LINEBACKER: Keep pass-rush contain on the quarterback

MEG LINEBACKER: Read pass, check the tan back, seam and hook.

STRONG SALLY

The strong Sally stunt is very similar to the strong squeeze. The same positions will be running the stunt. The strong end and the Mike linebacker will exchange gap and option responsibilities. We will not "red" out of the stunt. NOTE: In a "switch position," the Sam linebacker will exchange gap and option responsibilities with the end. On the pass, the Mike linebacker and the Sam linebacker will exchange pass responsibilities; Mike will have contain on the quarterback, and Sam will have the seam and hook.

TEAR

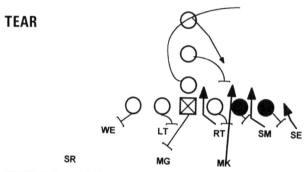

TACKLE: Stunt "A" gap

SAM LINEBACKER: Square up, "C" gap

STRONG END: Square up, "D" gap

MIKE LINEBACKER: Bust "B" gap

OPTION

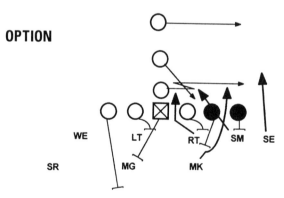

TACKLE: Stunt "A" gap, #1 option

SAM LINEBACKER: Go hard through the hip of the tackle, "B" gap, #1 on the option

STRONG END: "D" gap, #3 on option

MIKE LINEBACKER: Take the tackle on straight up and bounce to "C" gap, #2 on the option

POWER

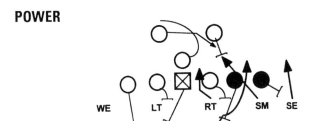

TACKLE: Stunt "A" gap

SAM LINEBACKER: Go hard through the hip of the tackle, "B" gap, keep outside leverage on the fullback

STRONG END: Square up, "D" gap

MIKE LINEBACKER: Take the tackle on straight up and bounce to "C" gap

DROP BACK

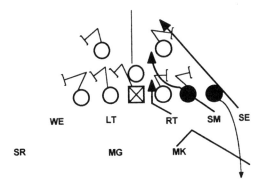

TACKLE: Stunt "A" gap, pass rush

SAM LINEBACKER: Go hard through the hip of the tackle "B," inside pass rush

STRONG END: Keep pass-rush contain on the quarterback

MIKE LINEBACKER: Read pass, check the tight end, seam and hook

WEAK SALLY

The weak Sally stunt is very similar to the weak squeeze. The same positions will be running the stunt. The Meg linebacker and the Sara linebacker will exchange gap, option, and pass responsibilities. We will not "red" out of the stunt. The Meg linebacker cannot hesitate when his key steps to the side of the stunt; instead, he should come hard. This stunt is not a slow read type of stunt.

TEAR

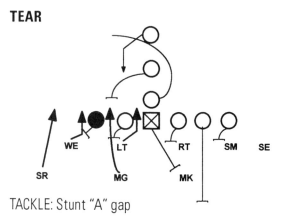

TACKLE: Stunt "A" gap

WEAK END: Square up, "C" gap

SARA LINEBACKER: Square up, "D" gap

MEG LINEBACKER: Bust "B" gap

OPTION

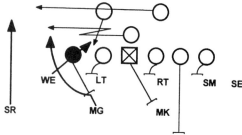

TACKLE: Stunt "A" gap, #1 option

WEAK END: Go hard through the hip of the tackle "B" gap, #1 on the option

SARA LINEBACKER: "D" gap, #3 on the option

MEG LINEBACKER: Take the tackle on straight up and bounce to "C" gap, #2 on the option

POWER

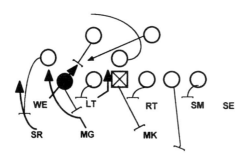

TACKLE: Stunt "A" gap

WEAK END: Go hard through the hip of the tackle "B" gap, keep outside leverage on the fullback

SARA LINEBACKER: Square up, "D" gap

MEG LINEBACKER: Take the tackle on straight up and bounce to "C" gap

SPRINT-OUT

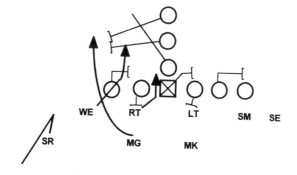

TACKLE: Stunt "A" gap, pass rush

WEAK END: Go hard through the hip of the tackle "B," inside pass rush

SARA LINEBACKER: Pass: seam and hook

MEG LINEBACKER: Keep pass-rush contain on the quarterback

FIST III MIKE AND MEG READ

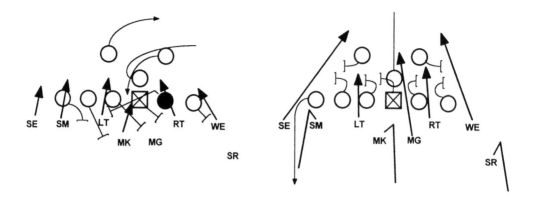

The Mike and Meg linebackers and the two tackles will be involved in this stunt. Just before the snap, the two inside linebackers will move up to the heels of the tackles. The linebacker should tap the tackle on the hip so as to move him to the outside shoulder of the offensive guard. The linebackers will read the helmet of the offensive center. The center will always block to one side of the ball, either right or left. When the center makes his step to his block, the linebacker to the opposite side of the block should stunt "A" gap. The linebacker to the side of the block will play his normal FIST III technique, with the exception of pass. If the play is a pass, the linebacker should drop to the "hole." The two outside linebackers should play everything the same as they would for FIST III, with the exception of pass, and drop to the seam and hook zones.

FIST III THUNDER/HOT

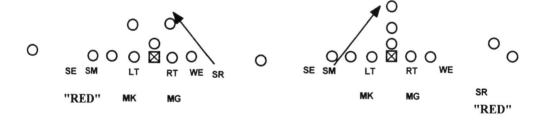

In this scenario, we will call two stunts, but will run only one of them. The linebacker will call off the stunt to the two-receiver side by yelling, "Red!"; remember, the two-receiver side will be the side of the color call. The stunt will be run to the one-receiver side.

FIST III MIKE AND MEG SPY

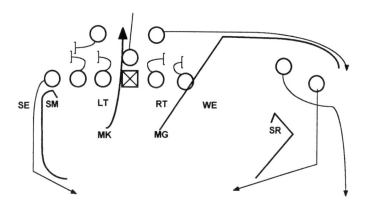

This stunt will be used only when the offensive play is a pass. If the play is something other than a pass, the normal FIST III technique will be used. When the play is a pass, the inside linebacker reads the "near back"; if the near back pass blocks, the linebacker should rush the passer. If the back runs a route, the linebacker should play man coverage on him—and he should not hesitate to get on the near back right away. He should jump the route on the offensive side of the line of scrimmage. The outside linebackers should play normal technique, with the exception of pass. When the play is a pass, they should drop to the seam and look for and play the inside route to their side first. If there is no inside route, they should look for crossing routes, and then play the routes to the outside.

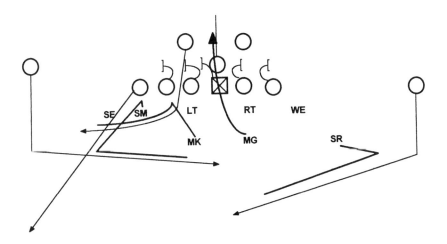

FIST III SNAKE

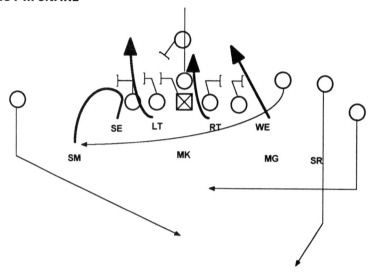

This stunt will be used only when the offensive play is a pass. If the play is something other than a pass, then normal FIST III technique will be employed. When the play is a pass, the defensive end to the one-receiver side should step into the offensive tackle as if he were pass rushing, and then step back and read the near back (the back to his side). If the back runs a route to his side, then the defensive end should play man coverage on him. The defensive end should not hesitate; rather, he should get on the near back right away and should jump the route on the offensive side of the line of scrimmage. If the back blocks, the defensive end should look for routes from the opposite side. The defensive tackles on the one-receiver side must get contain on the quarterback. The tackle on the two-receiver side should rush "A" gap. If the receiver set is balanced (double brown or tan), then we will go to the short field or game plan. (We may also stunt an inside linebacker.)

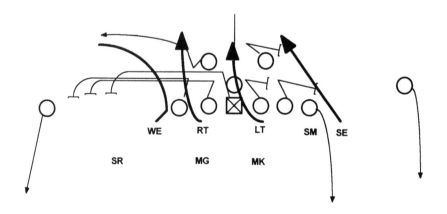

FIST III TWIST

The twist is run only on the open side; the end goes first to "B" gap, and the tackle goes behind to "C" gap and has contain.

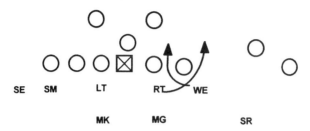

FIST III TWIST MIKE & MEG 1 GO

The inside linebacker on the one-receiver side stunts "A" gap; the outside linebacker has the seam and hook.

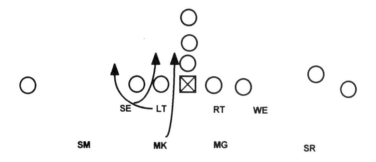

FIST III TWIST MIKE & MEG 2 GO

Both inside linebackers stunt "A" gap, and the outside linebackers have the seam and hook.

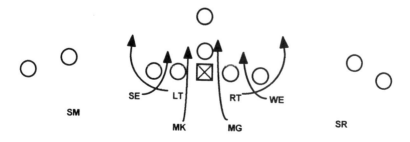

CHAPTER 12

Kicking Game

PUNT RETURNS, INTERCEPTIONS, FUMBLES, AND BLOCKED KICKS

We have four opportunities to score: (1) on an interception; (2) on a fumble; (3) on a blocked placekick; and (4) on a punt return. It has been said that in a close game, the deciding factors will be the kicking game and field position. We want to make good on every chance to score, or at least put the offense in position to score. When an opportunity to score occurs, we will set a "wall" return to the closest sideline. The reason we want to set our wall to the closest sideline is that after every down, the ball is placed somewhere between the hashes, making this area the site of the biggest concentration of offensive players. When the offensive team becomes the defensive team during a play, its players have to fan out and cover the field. On our wall returns, we want to set the wall quickly and to the point farthest away from the concentration of offensive players. On turnovers, fumbles, interceptions, and blocked kicks, we will set the wall on the fly. We will make a "bingo" call to the closest sideline: "Bingo left!" Everybody should get to the numbers of the side of the bingo call and set a wall. After making the bingo call, the returner must get to the wall, even if he has to give ground to do so. Once the returner is at the wall, he should turn it upfield, staying about a yard in bounds. An important coaching point that the players need to keep in mind—on any type of return—is that when they block on a return, they cannot block below the waist or from behind. Sometimes a "no block" is better than an attempt that results in a penalty.

PUNT RETURNS

We have three punt returns, each with a certain purpose, for situations that we may see during the course of a game. Our wall return is the return we use the most. Our middle return is used when the punter is kicking the ball low and deep. We will also use our middle return as a change-up. Our safe return will be used when teams are trying to kick the ball to the corner. We will also use our safe return whenever there might be a fake, or on bad-weather days, when we need to make sure we catch the ball.

WALL RETURN

Our players need to keep the line straight on the wall and also keep the distance between each other to four to five yards. When a player locates the ball, and the punt is a short kick, he should yell, "Short!" In that case, he should promptly get away from the ball; the best place to go is out of bounds. He should also let the player attacking the wall come to him; and he should hold a count before he pulls the trigger. If the ball is kicked to the other side of the opposite hash, the safety or the Sara linebacker should give a "Go" call, and the wall should move out to the near hash. The huddle for our punt-return team should be the same as our defensive huddle. With the exception of the two returners, they should be getting their depth and their alignment.

MIDDLE RETURN

Our middle return is very simple. The players simply need to remember to occupy and funnel to the outside. They should get their body between the offensive player and the middle of the field. They should also stay with their block as long as possible. Their alignment on the middle return is the same as it is on the wall return.

SAFE RETURN

The first thing we want to accomplish with our safe return is to stop any punt fake. Once the ball is punted, we need to catch the ball first, and then we will return the ball. The alignment of the safety and the halfbacks will depend on the strength of the punter's leg, as well as the punting team's field position. Our players need to remember the "10-yard rule." The distance between the halfbacks and the safety should be about 15 yards. The Sara and Sam linebackers should set two walls on the numbers to each side of the field. The return will be somewhat like a bingo call.

PUNT RETURN

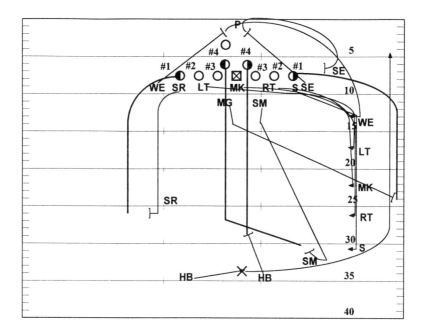

WEAK AND STRONG ENDS: Their alignment is outside of the #1 offensive player. Their responsibilities are to put pressure on the punter with a contain rush—to look for a bad snap or a mishandled snap. If they have a clear shot at the block, they should go for it, but they should make sure they don't miss it. If they are to the side of the return, they should circle and block the punter. As the defensive ends to the side away from the return, the weak end and the strong end are the last men on the wall.

SAFETY AND SARA LINEBACKER: Their alignment is head-up the #1 offensive player. The safety and the Sara linebacker will either be setting the wall or blocking the funnel man opposite the return. When setting the wall, they should release from the line of scrimmage as the punter starts his punting motion. They should get their width first and then go down the middle of the numbers. They should set the wall five to seven yards in front of the point where the ball was caught. Once the ball is caught by the returner, the wall should not be moved. The only exception to this is when the ball is kicked to the other side of the opposite hash, in which case the safety and the Sara linebacker should give a "Go" call. This call will move the wall to the hash. If #1 has a wide split, the alignment of the safety and the Sara linebacker will still be head-up.

LEFT AND RIGHT TACKLES: They should align on the inside shoulder of the #2 offensive player. At the snap, the tackles should stay on the line of scrimmage, check for a fake, and, as the punter starts his punting motion, release to the wall.

The tackles should get their width first and then go down the numbers to their position on the wall.

MIKE LINEBACKER: He should align head-up the offensive center. At the snap, Mike should stay on the line of scrimmage, check for the fake, and, as the punter starts his punting motion, release to the wall. He should get his width first and then go down the numbers to his position on the wall.

MEG LINEBACKER: He should align in "A" gap to the left side, as if we are going for a punt block. Just before the ball is snapped, he should back out to a depth of five yards. When the ball is snapped, the Meg linebacker should start to backpedal, looking for either a fake, a bad snap, or a short punt. If the punt is short, he should yell, "Short! Short!" and get away from the ball. If there is a bad snap, or the offense is running a fake punt, Meg should yell, "Fake! Fake!" as he reacts to the play. When the ball is punted and it is not short, he should open to the wall. He should run at an angle to the wall, passing through somewhere between the two tackles. Meg should block the first offensive player coming up the sideline. If no one comes, he should lead the return upfield.

SAM LINEBACKER: He should align in "A" gap to the left side, as if we are going for a punt block. Just before the ball is snapped, he should back out to a depth of five yards. When the ball is snapped, the Sam linebacker should start to backpedal, looking for either a fake, a bad snap, or a short punt. If the punt is short, he should yell, "Short! Short!" and get away from the ball. If there is a bad snap, or the offense is running a fake punt, Sam should yell, "Fake! Fake!" as he reacts to the play. When the ball is punted and it is not short, he should open to the wall. He should run at an angle to the wall to a point which is halfway between the safety and the punt returner. Sam should block the man most dangerous to the returner. If no one comes, he should lead the return up the wall.

RIGHT AND LEFT HALFBACKS: The depth of their alignment will depend on the ability of the punter. The distance between the right and the left halfback should be about 15 yards. One of the two halfbacks will be assigned to make the call that determines who is going to make the catch: "Me, me!" or "You, you!" Whoever catches the ball should fair catch any short ball and get away from any ball that cannot be caught. The halfback who is not catching the ball should position himself five to seven yards in front of the catch. He should also block the first man down in the path to the wall; if no one is there, he should return up the wall. The halfback making the catch should get to the wall, give ground if he needs to, but get to the wall and turn it upfield, keeping one yard from the boundary. The 10-yard rule comes into play anytime the ball is at our end of the field and the punter's leg could put the ball inside the 10-yard line. The halfbacks should stand on the 10-yard line, and any ball that they can catch in front of them should be fair caught or returned. On any ball that is over their head, they should signal for the fair catch and let the ball bound into the end zone.

MIDDLE RETURN

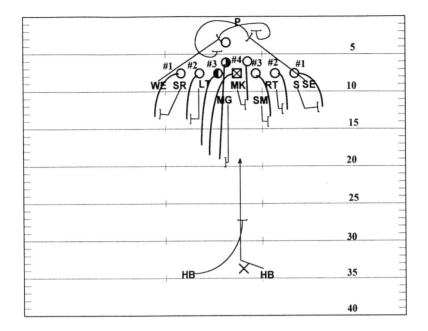

The middle return is very simple. The key is to occupy and funnel to the outside. Our players should get their body between the offensive players and the middle of the field. They should also stay with their block as long as possible. Our alignment is the same one we use on our wall return.

LEFT AND RIGHT ENDS: Same responsibilities as on the wall return, except the left end will block the punter and the right end will block the "up back."

SAFETY AND SARA LINEBACKER: They block #1.

LEFT AND RIGHT TACKLES: They block #2.

MIKE LINEBACKER: He blocks #4 on the right.

MEG LINEBACKER: He blocks either #3 or #4 on the left, whoever releases first.

SAM LINEBACKER: He blocks #3 on the right.

LEFT AND RIGHT HALFBACKS: The halfback who is not making the catch should move up and take the first man to the ball. The halfback who is making the return should try to move straight upfield. Once he breaks the first wave of the punt coverage, he should find clear sailing.

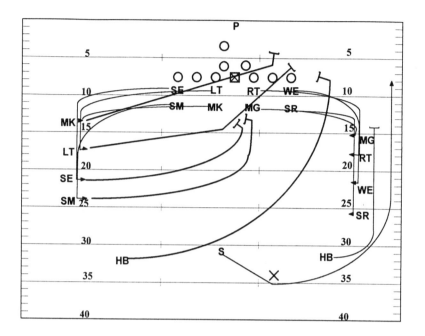

The first thing we want to accomplish with our safe return is to stop any punt fake. Once the ball is punted, we need to catch the ball first, and then return the ball. The alignment of the safety and the halfbacks will depend on the strength of the punter's leg, as well as the field position of the punting team. Players should remember the 10-yard rule. The distance between the halfbacks and the safety should be about 15 yards. The Sara and Sam linebackers will set two walls on the numbers to each side of the field. The return will be run somewhat like a bingo call.

PUNT BLOCK

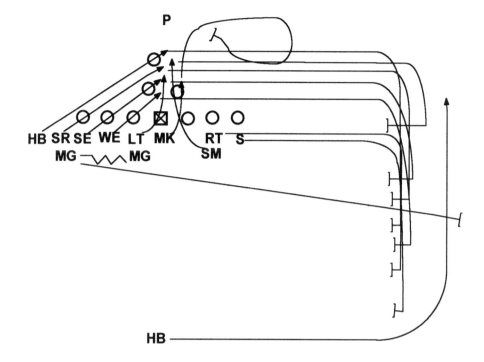

LEFT HALFBACK: Go for the block on the outside.

SARA LINEBACKER: Come inside the deep back for the block.

STRONG END: Come inside the back for the block.

WEAK END: Come through the guard's stance for the block.

LEFT TACKLE: Come through the hip of the center for the block.

MIKE LINEBACKER: Go through "A" gap for the block; if the ball is punted, block the punter on the return.

SAM LINEBACKER: Come off the hip of the Mike linebacker for the block.

RIGHT TACKLE: Look for the fake and keep contain on the punter. If the ball is punted, help set up the wall to the right.

SAFETY: Cover the end if he runs a pass route. If the ball is punted, keep contain on the punter and set up the wall to the right.

MEG LINEBACKER: Just before the snap, slide over to a position that is head-up the end. Cover the end if he runs a pass route. If the ball is punted, keep contain on the punter, go through the wall, and block the first man to the outside.

RIGHT HALFBACK: Fair catch the ball or run a return to the right.

If the punter gets the ball off, we will set a wall return to the right.

ALL-OUT PUNT BLOCK

P

HB SR SE WE LT MK RT MG S HB
SM

FIELD GOAL BLOCKS #1, #2, #3

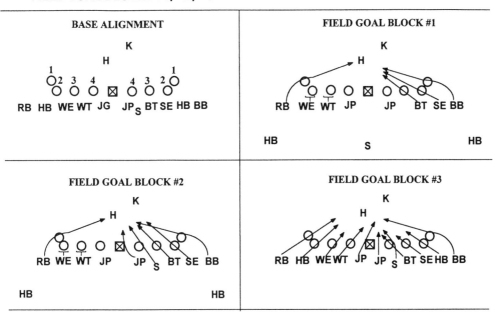

STRONG END (SE): The strong end is the second man in on the side of the block. At the snap, he should come hard through the hip of the offensive lineman and the inside foot of the "wingback." If he is blocked from either the inside or the outside, the strong end should bounce outside and look for the fake. The strong end should never assume that someone is going to block him. His charge and his mind must be focused on getting through untouched for the block.

BLOCK TACKLE (BT): The block tackle is the third man in on the side of the block. At the snap, he should come hard though the hip of the offensive lineman and the inside foot of the lineman to the outside. If he is blocked from either the inside or the outside, the block tackle should bounce outside and look for the fake. Like the strong end, he should never assume that someone is going to block him. His charge and his mind must be focused on getting through untouched for the block.

JUMPER (JP): The jumper alignment should be to either side of a line that runs from where the ball will be kicked to the middle of the goalpost. The jumper should time his jump with the kicker and the ball so that he will be able to block any low kick.

WEAK END AND WEAK TACKLE (WE/WT): Their alignment will be on the side opposite the block. They should hold their ground and look for a fake.

SAFETY (S): The safety should align in "B" gap on the side of the block. When the halfback makes the "move" call, the safety should drop to the middle third and look for the fake. The safety also has the option of returning the kick if it is short or blocked.

BLOCK BACK (BB): The block back is the primary block player we are sending for the kick. His alignment will always be on the outside, to the side of the block. At the snap, he should come hard through the hip of the wingback and go for the ball by laying out just in front of the kick point.

RETURN BACK (RB): The return back's alignment is on the outside, on the opposite side of the block. He has two responsibilities: (1) At the snap, he should run at the holder and position himself to stop the fake. He should not try to block the kick. (2) When the kick is blocked and it goes to the side or behind the kicker, he should pick up the ball and return it.

We utilize three different field goal blocks, called #1, #2, and #3. Field goal block #1 is the block that we will use most often. Field goal block #2 will be used when we want to put a little more pressure on the kicker and make something happen. Field goal block #3 is an all-out block, where we send everyone after the block. We will always align in our all-out block (field goal block #3) alignment and then shift to the block we are actually running.

FIELD GOAL BLOCK #1: When the ball is in the middle of the field, we will run the block to the right against a right-footed kicker (to the left against a left-footed kicker). When the ball is on the hash, the block should come from the open-field side.

FIELD GOAL BLOCK #2: On this block, we will run more blockers at the kicker from the block side. The safety and the jumper to the side of the block should go on the block. The halfbacks should play 1/2's coverage. The jumper should go through "A" gap, and the safety should go through "B" gap.

FIELD GOAL BLOCK #3: This block calls for everybody to take the gap to his inside and go for the block. The return back and the block back should come from the outside on either side.

KICKOFF

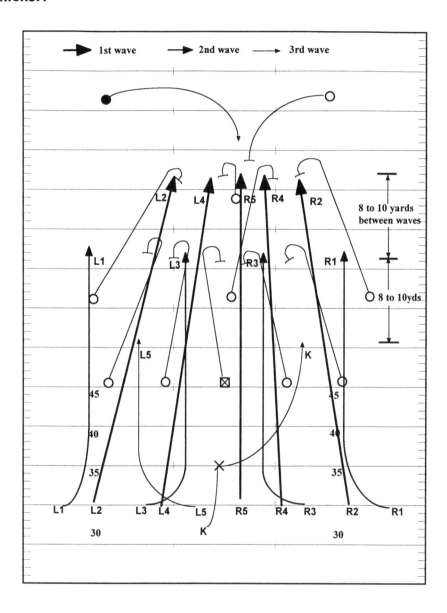

First wave: Flat out to the ball, 2's are responsible for contain, 4's and R5 stay on line with 2's.

Second wave: 1's come down the numbers, 3's inside of the hash; stay on line and trap the ball if the return breaks the first wave.

Third wave: L5 and the kicker are the safeties, halfway between the hash and the numbers; if the return breaks, the tackle must be made.

DEEP ONSIDE KICK

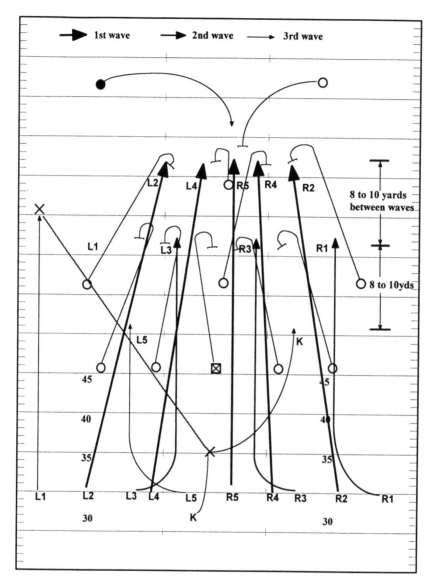

The deep onside kick is the same as our kickoff, except that the kicker kicks the ball to the boundary on the 35-yard line. The L1 runs flat out to the ball.

ONSIDE KICK

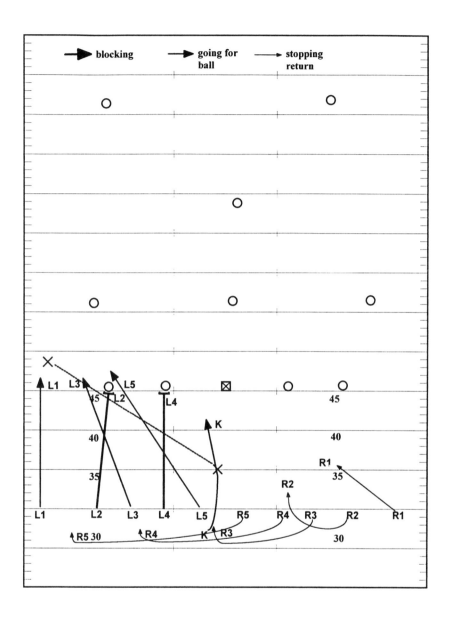

SCOUTING REPORT

TEAM: HARPER   **DATE: 11/9/96**

FORMATION: BLUE   **SET: "I" & SPLIT**

#44 #43
#23
#84 O O O ⊠ O O   #9

FORMATION: BROWN   **SET: "I' & HEAVY**

#44 O
#45 O
#84 O
O O O ⊠ O O   #23 O #9 O

FORMATION: GREEN   **SET: "I" & SPLIT**

#43   #44
#23
#8   #9
O O O ⊠ O O

FORMATION: BLUE/BROWN   #44 O   **SET: ACE**

#23   #8   #9
#84 O O O ⊠ O O   O   O

FORMATION: BLUE/TRIPS   #44 O   **SET: ACE**

#8   #23
O   O   #84 O O O ⊠ O O   #9 O

NOTES: GOAL LINE; BLACK, PINK BROWN, BLUE/BROWN AND MOTION
FROM ALL SET

**MOTION: BLUE TO BROWN AND BROWN TO BLUE, BLACK MOTION AND BLUE BROWN
MOTION TO TRIPS. BLACK SHORT MOTION, LEAD BLOCKER**

DEFENSIVE SCRIPT

	PERSONNEL					BACK-UPS		
POS.	NAME & YEAR		NO.	HT.	WT.	NO.	HT.	WT.
QB	J, ANDERSEN	FR.	#7	6'	206	#4	6'2"	195
RB	R, DAVIDSON	FR.	#44	5'10"	210	#31	5'10"	210
FB	SEAN BROWN	FR.	#45	5'10"	232	#43	5'9"	210
SE	JOHN LOWLOR	FR.	#23	6'	185	#1	6'	195
FL	TYWON MANNING	FR.	#8	5'5"	155			
TE	KWAN MERRIWEATHER	FR.	#84	6'3"	225			
ST	PAT HIGGENS	FR.	#78	6'8"	314			
SG	SAM WHEELER	FR.	#74	6'6"	340			
C	CHRIS BAZZELL	FR.	#64	6'4"	270			
WG	JOE CINQUEPALMI	SO.	#68	6'3"	280			
WT	CHRIS COALSON	FR.	#70	6'3"	280			

QB'S & THROWING HAND
STARTER   BACK-UPS
#7 RT.   #4 LT.

BEST BACK   #44 & #45

BEST RECEIVER #9 & #23

BEST LINEMAN #74 & #68

BEST PLAYER   #44 & #23

PUNTER & PUNTING FOOT
STARTER   BACK-UP
#12   #26

KICKER & KICKING FOOT
STARTER   BACK-UP
#16 RT.   #12 RT.

LONG SNAPPER
PUNTS   FIELD GOALS
#55   #65

UPBACK   HOLDER
#41   #4

KICKOFF

#1○   #21○
○   ○
○   ○
○ ○ ○ ○ ○

wedge center return
#1 good return man

PUNT

#12 ○   #43 comes in
           at upback on
#41 ○   fake punt
#33 #81
○ ○ ○ ○ ○ ○ ○
       #55

FIELD GOAL

#16 ○
       ○ #4
#33   #21
○
○ ○ ○ ● ○ ○ ○
       #65

They will huddle and break to
the l.o.s. away from the ball, the
center, kicker and holder are
over the ball on fake.

RUN PLAYS

TEAM HARPER

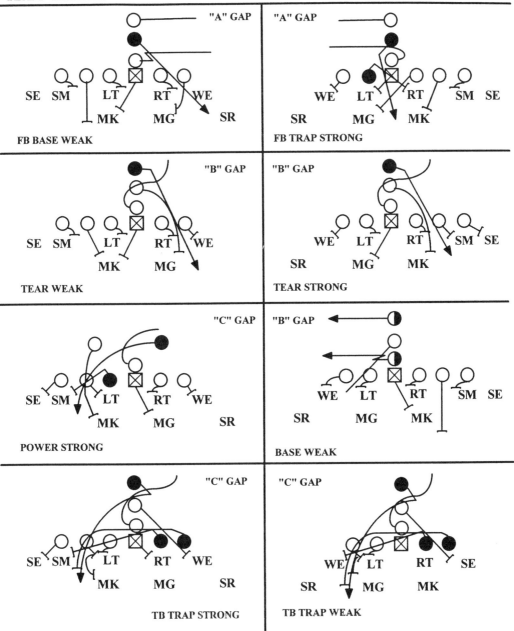

"A" GAP

FB BASE WEAK

"A" GAP

FB TRAP STRONG

"B" GAP

TEAR WEAK

"B" GAP

TEAR STRONG

"C" GAP

POWER STRONG

"B" GAP

BASE WEAK

"C" GAP

TB TRAP STRONG

"C" GAP

TB TRAP WEAK

RUN PLAYS

TEAM HARPER

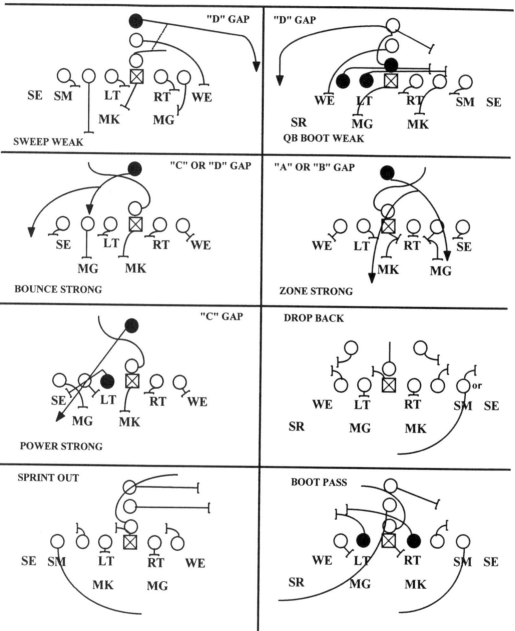

"D" GAP

SE SM   LT   RT WE
MK   MG

SWEEP WEAK

"D" GAP

WE   LT   RT   SM SE
SR   MG   MK

QB BOOT WEAK

"C" OR "D" GAP

SE   LT   RT WE
MG   MK

BOUNCE STRONG

"A" OR "B" GAP

WE   LT   RT   SE
MK   MG

ZONE STRONG

"C" GAP

SE   LT   RT   WE
MG   MK

POWER STRONG

DROP BACK

WE   LT   RT   SM SE
SR   MG   MK

or

SPRINT OUT

SE SM   LT   RT   WE
MK   MG

BOOT PASS

WE   LT   RT   SM SE
SR   MG   MK

PASS PLAYS

TEAM   HARPER

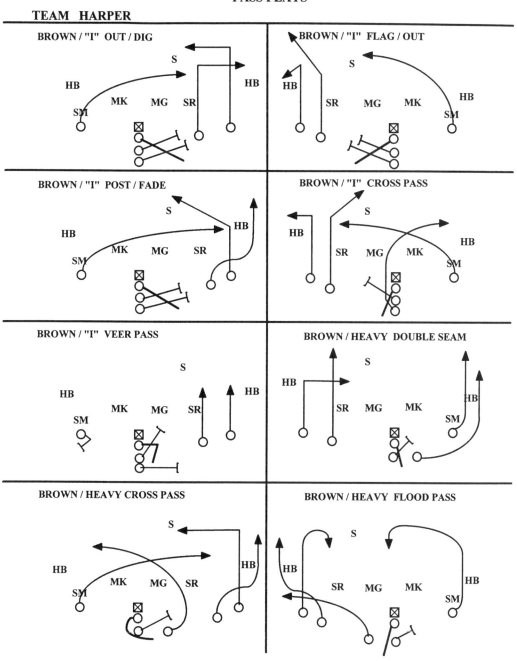

BROWN / "I" OUT / DIG

BROWN / "I" FLAG / OUT

BROWN / "I" POST / FADE

BROWN / "I" CROSS PASS

BROWN / "I" VEER PASS

BROWN / HEAVY DOUBLE SEAM

BROWN / HEAVY CROSS PASS

BROWN / HEAVY FLOOD PASS

PASS PLAYS

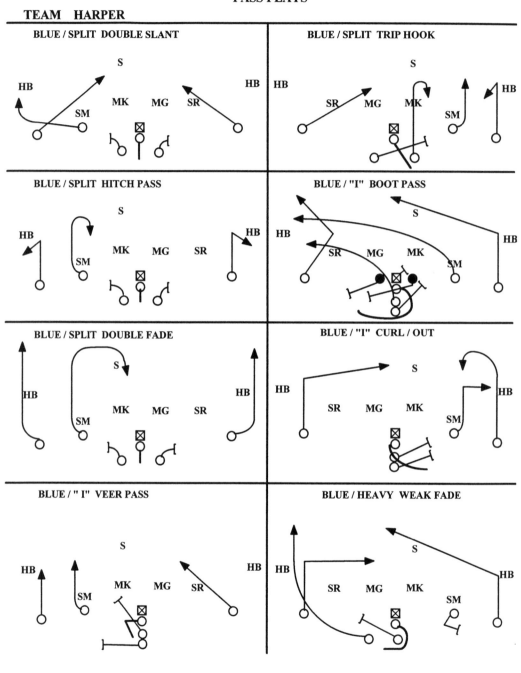

BLUE / SPLIT DOUBLE SLANT

BLUE / SPLIT TRIP HOOK

BLUE / SPLIT HITCH PASS

BLUE / "I" BOOT PASS

BLUE / SPLIT DOUBLE FADE

BLUE / "I" CURL / OUT

BLUE / " I" VEER PASS

BLUE / HEAVY WEAK FADE

PASS PLAYS

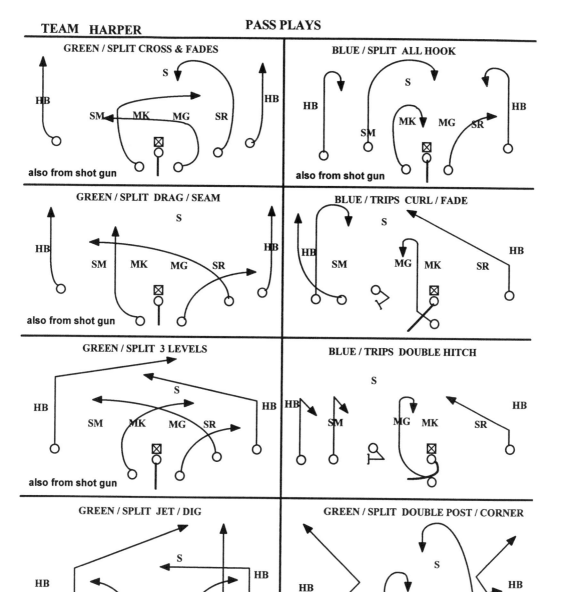

GREEN / SPLIT CROSS & FADES

HB · S · HB · SM · MK · MG · SR

also from shot gun

BLUE / SPLIT ALL HOOK

HB · S · HB · SM · MK · MG · SR

also from shot gun

GREEN / SPLIT DRAG / SEAM

HB · S · HB · SM · MK · MG · SR

also from shot gun

BLUE / TRIPS CURL / FADE

HB · S · HB · SM · MG · MK · SR

GREEN / SPLIT 3 LEVELS

HB · S · HB · SM · MK · MG · SR

also from shot gun

BLUE / TRIPS DOUBLE HITCH

HB · S · HB · SM · MG · MK · SR

GREEN / SPLIT JET / DIG

HB · S · HB · SM · MK · MG · SR

also from shot gun

GREEN / SPLIT DOUBLE POST / CORNER

HB · S · HB · SM · MK · MG · SR

also from shot gun

GOAL LINE PLAYS

TEAM HARPER

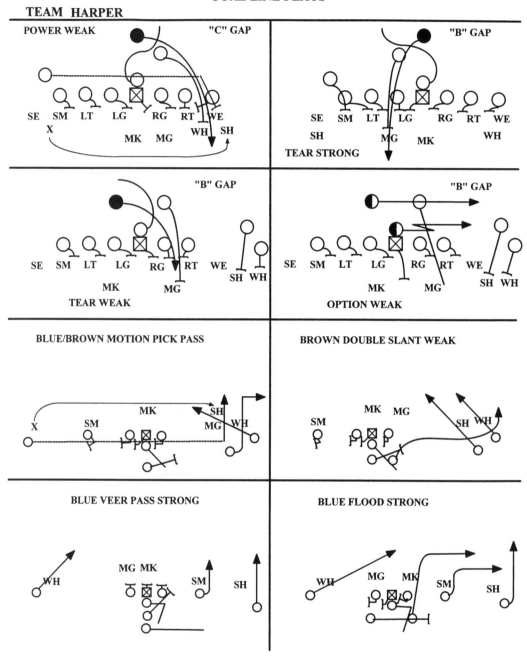

POWER WEAK   **"C" GAP**

SE   SM   LT   LG   RG   RT   WE
X   MK   MG   WH   SH

"B" GAP

SE   SM   LT   LG   RG   RT   WE
SH   MG   MK   WH
TEAR STRONG

"B" GAP

SE   SM   LT   LG   RG   RT   WE
MK   MG   SH   WH
TEAR WEAK

"B" GAP

SE   SM   LT   LG   RG   RT   WE
MK   MG   SH   WH
OPTION WEAK

BLUE/BROWN MOTION PICK PASS

X   SM   MK   SH
MG   WH

BROWN DOUBLE SLANT WEAK

SM   MK   MG   SH   WH

BLUE VEER PASS STRONG

WH   MG   MK   SM   SH

BLUE FLOOD STRONG

WH   MG   MK   SM   SH

COLLEGE OF DUPAGE

DEFENSIVE SCRIPT

PREPARATION VS: _____

DATE: _____ SITUATION: _____ PRACTICE: _____ TIME: _____

DEFENSIVE FRONT	COVERAGE		FORMATION	PLAY
1.		1.		
2.		2.		
3.		3.		
4.		4.		
5.		5.		
6.		6.		
7.		7.		
8.		8.		
9.		.9.		
10.		10.		
11.		11.		
12.		12.		
13.		13.		
14.		14.		
15.		15.		
16.		16.		
17.		17.		
18.		18.		
19.		19.		
20.		20.		
21.		21.		
22.		22.		
23.		23.		
24.		24.		
25.		25.		
26.		26.		
27.		27.		
28.		28.		
29.		29.		
30.		30.		

RUN SHOT CHART

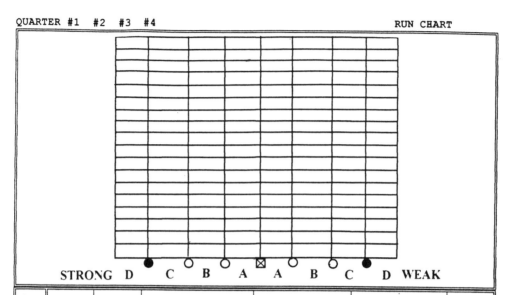

STRONG　D　　C　　B　　A　　A　　B　　C　　D　WEAK

#	D/D	GAIN	FORMATION\SET	ACTION	GAP\STRENGTH	BACK
1						
2						
3						
4						
5						
5						
6						
7						
8						
9						
10						
11						
12						
13						
14						
15						
16						
17						
18						

PASS SHOT CHART

QUARTER #1 #2 #3 #4   PASS CHART

outside 1/3		middle 1/3		outside 1/3	
crease	curl	hole		curl	crease
flat	seam	hook	hook	seam	flat

● ○ ○ ⊠ ○ ○ ●

#	D/D	GAIN	FORMATION\SET	ACTION	ROUTE\STRENGTH	REC.
1						
2						
3						
4						
5						
6						
7						
8						
9						
10						
11						
12						
13						
14						
15						
16						
17						
18						

Joe Roman enjoyed a long and illustrious career as defensive coordinator at the College of DuPage in Glen Ellyn, Illinois. For 23 years, beginning in 1975, Roman's coaching was a major reason DuPage won 75 percent of its football games.

En route to a composite mark of 182-61, the Chaparrals played in 14 bowl games and won 10 of them; won 12 State Junior College championships; and won 36 consecutive games at one point, setting a National Junior College Athletic Association record. From 1986 to 1996, the College of DuPage racked up a record of 107-22, won eight consecutive state championships, and was ranked in the top 10 in the nation seven times. During that same span, DuPage's team defense finished in the top 10 in the nation eight times. In 1995, the Chaparrals' defense enjoyed its most successful season, giving up only 51 points in 12 games (4.2 points per game). On the way to finishing No. 1 in the country in team defense, the Chaparrals held their opponents to an average of 132 yards of total offense per game (35 yards rushing, 97 yards passing).

Prior to taking the post at DuPage, Roman coached high school football for four years. During graduate school at Wayne State University, Roman coached the linebackers and helped the team to a 9-2 record and a berth in the NAIA Mineral Water Bowl. Roman graduated from Moorhead State University in Minnesota in 1969, where he lettered in football and wrestling.

After the College of DuPage announced in 1996 that it was dropping its football program, Roman spent a year coaching high school football. In the spring of 1998, he retired from teaching and moved to Chandler, Arizona, where he became linebackers coach at Mesa Community College. Following the 1998 regular season, the Thunderbirds advanced to the Valley of the Sun Bowl, where they lost to Garden City (KS) Community College, 17-14.

Mesa CC's season mark of 7-4 brought the overall record of the teams that Roman has helped coach to 227-70.

ADDITIONAL FOOTBALL
RESOURCES FROM

ADDITIONAL FOOTBALL RESOURCES FROM

COACHES CHOICE™

ADDITIONAL FOOTBALL RESOURCES FROM

COACHES ≡ CHOICE ™

MORE TITLES FROM THE 101 DRILLS SERIES

O F F E N S E

101 Quarterback Drills
Steve Axman
1998 ▪ 128 pp ▪ Paper ▪ ISBN 1-57167-195-1 ▪ $16.95

101 Ways to Run the Option
Tony DeMeo
1999 ▪ 140 pp ▪ Paper ▪ ISBN 1-57167-368-7 ▪ $16.95

101 Receiver Drills
Stan Zweifel
1998 ▪ 128 pp ▪ Paper ▪ ISBN 1-57167-191-9 ▪ $16.95

D E F E N S E

101 Defensive Back Drills
Ron Dickerson and James A. Peterson
1997 ▪ 120 pp ▪ Paper ▪ ISBN 1-57167-089-0 ▪ $16.95

101 Linebacker Drills
Jerrry Sandusky and Cedric X. Bryant
1997 ▪ 120 pp ▪ Paper ▪ ISBN 1-57167-087-4 ▪ $16.95

101 Defensive Line Drills
Mark Snyder
1999 ▪ 120 pp ▪ Paper ▪ ISBN 1-57167-372-5 ▪ $16.95

TO PLACE YOUR ORDER OR FOR A FREE CATALOG:

U.S. customers call
TOLL FREE: (800) 327-5557
or visit our website at
www.coacheschoice-pub.com
or FAX: (217) 359-5975
or write
COACHES CHOICE™
P.O. Box 647, Champaign, IL 61824-0647